A

PHILOSOPHICAL INQUIRY

RESPECTING THE ABOLITION

OF

CAPITAL PUNISHMENT.

BY JAMES FOULHOUZE.

Reddite quæ sunt Cæsaris Cæsari—Et quæ sunt Dei Deo.—Matt. xxii. 21.

PHILADELPHIA:

URIAH HUNT, 101 MARKET STREET.

1842.

A Philosophical Inquiry Respecting the Abolition of Capital Punishment
by James Foulhouze

A Cornerstone Book
Published by Cornerstone Book Publishers
An Imprint of Michael Poll Publishing

Cornerstone Book Publishers
New Orleans, LA

First Cornerstone Edition - 2019

This is a photographic reproduction of the 18423 edition of this work.
www.cornerstonepublishers.com

ISBN:978-1-61342-333-2

MADE IN THE USA

TO THE VENERABLE SOCIETY OF FRIENDS IN THE STATE OF PENNSYLVANIA.

GENTLEMEN:

As I journeyed through this immense vale of grief and trouble, in which man runs but a short period of his immortal career, and in which so many evils besiege him on every side, because things are not as they ought to be, and in accordance with the intended designs of a benevolent Creator, I met with some members of your unostentatious society; and my intercourse proved, not long after, much more profitable than I had even dared to expect, for I found in them, what I had looked for in vain among many other societies, Good sense and Liberal ideas united with a practical virtue and an active philanthropy.

Such a discovery was a precious one for me, and I made it a pleasurable duty to investigate attentively the tenets of a society, the members of which were so intimately acquainted with the most correct principles of civil morality, and so admirably bound to each other by the sweet ties of a brotherly love.

Now, as I advanced in that useful investigation, I saw that you could not help being what you are, since one of the most respected of your wise founders, William Penn, had regulated your society so as to keep the genius of Good always busy and cheerful in its bosom, and to force the genius of Evil to tremble and bend, at all times, before his prudent and truly equitable legislation.

Equally adverse to the spirit of mysticism, the ambition of which is to enslave the mind, and also to the spirit of domination, which tends to destroy civil liberty, that very great and honest man laid the foundation of a government for which he legislated, upon this holy and solid ground, that the executive power and the people should respect each other sincerely and practically, as, in his well digested opinions, Liberty without obedience leads to disorder, and Obedience without liberty, constitutes a mere state of bondage.

Consequently, an impartial justice and a rational freedom were the chief ends of his administration. He would not multiply the number of judges, lest he should, by so doing, aid injustice in its machinations, and retard the expectations of probity; but ordered that every trial should be conducted so as to secure promptly the due of each one. Authority was respected and obeyed on the one side; and, on the other, the rights of the citizens firmly but calmly defended. No dangerous revolutions could be feared, because all were taught that of all the means to be used to obtain redress, Rebellion was the worst.

On another hand, his administration meddled not with religion. Every man, whether he belonged to his creed or not, enjoyed the same political and civil rights with his disciples. Public morals had been made by him so perfectly independent of his religious doctrines, that the law never interfered with the tenets of the other Christian or non-christian denominations, but acted always in an uncontrovertible accordance with the code of nature expounded by Universal reason.

But, if virtue was the main object of his pursuits, if he spared neither instructions nor efforts to render it acceptable, and make its success certain within the limits of his province; he did not, however, despair of vice, and would still less permit his fellow citizens to stamp it with the seal of an irremediable degradation; for his enlightened mind had ascertained, like that of Pascal, that man is susceptible of becoming good as well as he is liable to fall into evil.

Thus, his criminal code breathed a wholesome air of morality, the end of which was to render justice perfectly commutative. It provided for the safety of society, and supported also the interests of those who had been personally injured by a misdemeanor which exposed the offender to punishment. The premises of a jail were not made a sewer into which an ill understood civilization might throw its convicts, or a selfish institution, the authors of which could trample upon the sacred rights of an injured party, and satisfy a mere feeling of revenge; but a place of correction in which such as should be condemned by the law, should repair with the produce of the hard labour imposed upon them, the wrongs which they had caused, whilst their confinement would secure society, and inflict a punishment adequate to the transgression.

Such a legislation, I understand, could not suit men whose spirit inclined to a merciless absolutism, and whose thoughts were controlled by a religious egotism. But it was well calculated to answer the purpose of a nation truly desirous of progressing towards an improved state of civilization.

No doubt but it will be appreciated and cherished at a period which, I am pleased to believe, is not very remote; but, if ever a society consents to adopt it, it should place at the head of its beneficent reformers, the immortal William Penn.

Then, to whom but to you, Gentlemen, the zealous supporters of his excellent philosophy, should I offer this book, which is, chiefly, an earnest vindication of the philanthropical principles which he never ceased to advocate?

Perhaps I ought to have begged of you to let it appear under your good auspices, before I decided to publish it? But, if I was sure, on the one hand, that you would not decline granting me such a favour, though in some of my political and religious views I may not be entirely of your opinion; I was, on the other, afraid, lest some persons would suppose that I was actuated by another motive than that of a disinterested philanthropy, and, therefore, without complying with the usual formality, I resolved to present my work to you, as a tribute of gratitude to William Penn, whose doctrines have been as serviceable to me as they are dear to you,

GENTLEMEN,

Of whom I will always be a sincere admirer
And truly devoted servant,

JAMES FOULHOUZE.

ERRATA.

Page 12, line 11—for *theoretical* read *theocratical.*
" 48, " 6—for *prison alleviated* read *prison be alleviated.*
" 50, " 7—for *judicial murders* read *a judicial murder.*
" 71, " 25—for *shu* read *shut.*
" 124, " 40—for *are, indeed,* read *are, often.*

INTRODUCTION.

Ere the sacred fire of liberty was rekindled on earth, and ere the spirit of those nations which were to set an example to the whole world, was animated by it, Cruelty used to walk along with Barbarism its natural cause, between Ignorance and Tyranny, the contemptible guides of both; reason and philosophy were powerless; Christianity itself, because it had either fallen into the hands of proud and ambitious conquerors, or been accepted by men still barbarous, was, altogether, misunderstood, misconstrued, misrepresented. So, the cross of Jesus, which ought to rise triumphantly over mankind, and free them from bondage, became truly formidable, when grafted upon the crowns of those emperors and kings whose subjects, accustomed to fear and obey, read but severe laws in the code of mercy which had been enacted by their Saviour and sealed with his blood.

Indeed, their rulers dared not, through respect for the God who had suffered upon it, and whose religion they professed, use the cross as an instrument of death for criminals; but they substituted for it other torments not less cruel, not less excruciating; so that it may be said, that, whilst they boasted of their belief in Christ, they endeavoured to find out the best means to torture mankind.

The poetical enthusiasm of the Jewish prophets animated the arid prose of their codes. They erected, in the middle of their cities, between the temples consecrated to the mild Reformer of our kind and the civil monuments of the evangelical restoration, a set of those tormenting machines with which our Bible threatens sinners. Christian priests, whom a daily meditation upon the peaceful doctrines of the gospel preached by them, and a more intimate acquaintance with the feelings of Jesus, ought to inspire with ideas of forgiveness and thoughts of mercy, authorized this barbarous disposition of civil governments, by erecting ecclesiastical tribunals to judge and punish, with an equal severity, such persons whom they pleased to consider and accuse as religious dissenters.

Every where, death became the last or rather the only argument, both of lawgivers against social crimes, and of synods against heresies. Whether Catholic or Protestant, every Christian nation obeyed the raging control of this diabolical confederacy; and, up to a not very remote period, the annals of their civil conventions, as well as of their practical belief, seem to have been written, in many pages, by the bloody hands of public executioners.

Let us go back, mentally, to one hundred years from this time, and what shall we have to contemplate in those horrid places where criminals and heretics were brought to pass, under the blows of a tyrannical or priestly justice, the last hours of their execrated lives? Racks, upon which the limbs of the accused were either dislocated or subjected to excruciating pains, for the purpose of forcing the sufferer to a confession, and converting these very confessions into a source of new accusations; for the question was usually the forerunner of death. Again, what do we see? Quick-fires overspread with the smothering dust of brimstone, that the cries of grief and pain might be stifled, more surely, amidst burning coals:—red-hot iron bars, upon which bodies, still breathing, were given up to inhuman executioners, and felt their broken nerves and bones start between the lacerating teeth of pincers dipped in a horrible mixture of blood, pitch and tar:—four horses driven to madness, whipped purposely towards the four corners of a blood-damp square, that they might carry off, at the same time, the four main limbs of a man tightly tied to their tails, and leave but a disgusting trunk behind:—wheels, the evolutions of which caused successively the breaking of every nerve, every artery, every bone; and never stopped but to secure, for a herculean club, the last blow which was to be inflicted, in the name of a mocking mercy, on the panting breast of the victim! Such, I say, was the sight then exhibiting, for the punishment of a few and the instruction of the many! Christian judges ordered it to benefit Christian spectators; and these, a circumstance not less shameful to relate, bore it patiently—ran to it as to a theatrical performance. They spoke with horror of the dreadful persecutions which some pagan emperors had ordered against their forefathers, considered several of the Roman prefects as the very instruments of hell armed against Christ, cursed the memory of those bloody tyrants, compared them to the most barbarous of those man-eaters whose very name caused their hearts to shudder; and yet, they allowed their legislation to be sanguinary, and countenanced the most murderous auto-dafies! . . . . .

No: the most ruthless edicts of the Roman prefects were perhaps not more to be censured than the refined cruelties of the Christian Inquisition; and the most atrocious punishments inflicted among barbarous nations, do not offer us with any precedents beyond the hideous cruelty of which the criminal justice of our Christian societies has not gone. Let any man take this remark into consideration, and he will admit that it is actually established upon an uncontrovertible truth. Nations, no matter what their creed was, have to consent, that their religious and civil codes have been more or less stained with blood.

It is, therefore, their duty to rebel against a disgraceful past; to reform their criminal legislation whilst they tend to a sincere religious toleration among themselves. Science and reason, supported by good faith, tell them that an infinite distance has been left between heaven and earth, God and man, the church and the state, and, consequently, that there is no similarity between a guilty citizen and a departed sinner; that the torments of the life to come are no paradigm for the punishments which society has to inflict, in this world, upon its offenders.

Some priests, perhaps, or divines, who are yet endeavouring to keep from an utter ruin their faith in many superannuated doctrines, will abide still by the theoretical notions which caused our forefathers to part, in many important instances, from reason and justice; but they, as well as all those who stand out, with them, in their opinion, are evidently in the rear of the social progress: they live like slaves among freemen; they obey, blindly, unqualified rulers; grope along the unsafe path of suppositions; sacrifice daily their noblest and most sacred rights upon the altar of fear; and would let the world fall again into the abyss of dark ages, if the spirit of those unhappy times, during which error prevailed, tyranny reigned and the human kind trembled before it, had no other obstacle to overcome but their inthralled fidelity and unenlightened virtue.

It is no more a question to ascertain that which has been before our time; but to know what is to be done now; for, like individuals, nations cannot retrace their steps. The chance of working their own ruin, should they hasten too rashly along the road lately opened by a sanguine civilization, is no motive for them to stop; whilst they are bound necessarily to perish, if they consented, through either awe or coercion, to slacken their intended progress towards a better condition. All that which is good in itself will remain, or, at least, re-appear amidst the fragments and wrecks which coming changes are to heap confusedly together, because, like truth, good is imperishable; but whatever is wrong or bad, shall either be made right or undone, because our kind has an irresistible tendency to improve and better itself. So, priests, lawgivers, philosophers, all must make up their minds to obey this truly philanthropical impulsion, go a head, as it were, with this grand legislative reformation.

They should, I say: but will they? it is doubtful. Mankind, however alike all its members appear, is made out of very heterogeneous parts. Contradiction breathes in them naturally. Let one of them utter a thought, an opinion, and many others will immediately question and perhaps reject it! We live, it seems, but to suspect each other, to keep up envy, pride, selfishness; and thus, the freedom of thought and the power of speech, those precious elements of happiness, which were handed by God to society, in the beginning; have become as many means of perdition, when grasped by individuality. On the one part, many priests, whose sublime mission is to preach for the support of the beneficial doctrines which Nature teaches every where, and to use this as a faithful interpreter of truth, and the most potent auxiliary of Revelation, seem, on the contrary, to doubt it: nay, they consider it as a dangerous foe, despise it without motives, provoke it with bitterness, because philosophy worships and invokes it. Indeed, this mode of proceeding is not right; and nothing, in my opinion, would be more laughable than a sermon intended to impair the ascendency of natural wisdom over our minds, if man was allowed to laugh at that which, either directly or indirectly, relates to the sacred cause of heaven.

But, on the other part, many philosophers are, by no means, wiser or more moderate. Their intellect, irritated by the obstacles which priesthood is sometimes pleased to raise before them, thinks not but of triumphing over this skilful, cavilling, ambitious competitor, as they call it; and they wage an incessant war against it, without caring about the scandals to be originated by such contests, or inquiring, before hand, whether the rights of reason so defended, will not, soon or late, secure a complete victory for depravity; whether nations thus *Voltairized* or *Paynified* will not finish by parting both from God and social order, whilst they are taught to dislike both their priests and their religious practices.

So philosophy badly conceived is not less perilous than theology wrongly used; both may bring forth the same evils, and lead to equal abuses or calamities. Which intermediary power shall, by coming peaceful and strong between them, maintain impartially the sway of reason, and free religion from danger? that of lawgivers.

Unhappily, these have, for many centuries past, misunderstood their duty, and, therefore, filled up their codes with anomalies not less ridiculous than hazardous. Such as they are, they exhibit a mere compilation of edicts, statutes, and ordinances, which oppose and contradict each other; of axioms foes and friends, at the same time, of civil liberty; of principles semi-religious, semi-atheistical, which, like the quarrelling atoms of Descartes, pursue and catch each other at random; what for?—to mix confusedly and bring forth an incomprehensible world on which, after a given number of years, Truth and Falsehood, Good and Evil, Vice and Virtue, Religion and Incredulity, are to be seen under arms, or fighting together scandalously.

Indeed, from such a monument of human frailty, we should neither be astonished at all those imperfections with which our present social systems abound, nor complain of the slow march of the reformation which we stand in need of! its triumph amidst and over so many intricacies cannot be immediate. It is enough, if it gains something every day; if it surmounts, here, an obstacle; and vanquishes, there, some of its opponents; for, by dint of success, it will, at last, grow powerful and liberal. Every social crisis will leave it some new laurels to gather, as every prudent and rational law to be enacted, will be, for it, another precious inheritance to welcome. To spring, thus, and grow under the beneficent shades of peace, is, by far, better than to conquer amidst the darkness of revolutions, and reign over ruins.

However happy may, at last, be a nation in which a violent political commotion has prevailed, and changed the form of its government, there will, always, live a sad remembrance of its past miseries, which will cruelly impair its sensations of felicity, whilst it causes it to doubt whether it has acquired them legitimately. On the contrary, a State, of which the improvements have been the work of time, and public opinion gradually reformed, will see its citizens enjoying, without either fear or remorse, the good legislation which rules and protects them.

Then, far from the councils of nations may those men be who think too quickly, and act too sensitively. Like the torrent which rolls rapidly along the flowery sides of a mountain, of which the summit is crowned with icy snow, the symbol of wisdom, and the basis rests upon a rock, the image of strength, they appear grand, seduce, persuade, hurry away with them any thing which they touch; but, at the end of their gigantic and glorious course, they fall tumultuously, together with their works, into the abyss which opens to devour them, and nothing is left, after their conquests, but a vaporous, wan, death-looking mist which floats tremulously over the dreadful chasm in which they lose themselves for ever.

We must prefer to them those calm and composed, though energetic, strong minded men, whose thoughts drop slowly, but efficaciously over society, like a spring dew over the earth; and flow on every side, among their fellow-beings whom they revivify, like the wholesome waters of a modest source which, from the remotest parts of a valley, purl gently, through all the cuts of the meadows and gardens below. Indeed, their labour is neither so dazzling nor showy, but it is sweeter, livelier, surer.

May this inquiry, which I decide to publish through a philanthropical motive, work its way among men, and be conducive to the reformation of our criminal code, so that neither God nor man should blame it! My thoughts are those of a sincere mind: and my feelings such as sincerity dictates; any thing which I see around me, such as religious systems, manners, doctrines, prejudices, I respect; because all are laudable in some points, and, sometimes, may be useful; but, as they all depend upon men whose views are often imperfect, and opinions controvertible, one may investigate, refute, weaken, nay, cause them to pass away, provided his arguments depart at no time, either from moderation or good will; and do always abide with reason, which is the best support of truth.

That such must the character of mine be, the reader will admit, when I tell him that I am first of all, a Christian; then, a logician; and, lastly, a politician or jurisprudent, inasmuch as I have paid the constitution and laws of our country that careful attention which every good citizen owes them.

Therefore, if I speak of Christianity like a philosopher, of philosophy like a Christian, or of politics and law like a Christian philosopher, no one should either wonder at it, or complain of me. Man cannot use the language of faith, which rests upon mysteries, without displeasing philosophers a little, nor move freely within the limits of reason, which knows of no other law but that of nature, without hurting more or less the theological propensities of believers; and, still less, become the discreet Aristarch now of divines, now of philosophers, without seeming to teach politicians whose duty it is to protect both religion and reason.

Such is the susceptibility of human understanding, that it takes all sorts of forms, according to its primary education, or the tendency which qualifies it in its various positions. Some men, sincerely attached to the Christian creed, but rather too exclusive in their views, pretend that our Bible is the only criterion of truth, build upon it every religious or civil theory, solve confidently, with the help of its texts, not less pliable than numberless, the most intricate questions of social order, and swear upon it, in any case or time. Hence the sanguinary code of the Spanish Inquisition, of Calvin at Geneva, of Cromwell in England; the blue book of the puritanical reformation in some of the united provinces of British America; the massacres of the Huguenots under the reign of Charles the Ninth, and the revocation of the edict of Nantes in France.

Others, disciples of Nature, and determined such to remain, handle with an incredible boldness that book which Jews and Christians attribute to a special inspiration from God, censure it bitterly, deny its authority over society; of which, the inalienable rights, they say, rest unconditionally upon equality and reciprocity, as they are taught by the law of Nature. Hence the practical atheism of the French convention, and the dangerous theism imagined by some politicians.

I will blame neither of these extremes; for, to believe is, by no means, an act of our intellect, but a spontaneous feeling of our heart; whilst, to disbelieve may be either an error of our mind, or an absence of impulsion; and no one, except God, can decide whether the believer or unbeliever is wrong in his political notions. Hence this seemingly blameable, though truly religious axiom: *Upon the mysterious silence of God does actually rest the religious doubt and the inviolable liberty of man!*

But if I owe respect to both parties, I can, also, examine freely the principles of both, and endeavour to demonstrate that both have erred, so far as concerns the momentous question which I am to discuss. Positive and accurate statements of all the biblical, political, philosophical facts and doctrines which men have either gathered or taught, about capital punishment, laid before me, when I made it a duty to study, analyze and estimate them for the sake of information. A sincere disciple of Descartes, in whose mind a true faith in the Christian religion, united with a rational confidence in his natural powers and experience of life, I have, alternately, placed myself far from man, and far from God, to enjoy the pleasure of coming back to both; fully convinced, that if I was about to hurt some notions of my fellow beings, I would neither lie to myself nor to my Maker.

So, caring but little about what the world or the church may say, I performed my task, which I divide into two very distinct parts; the first of which comprises a metaphysical, biblical and religious examination of the subject; the second, a philosophical, civil and practical delineation of it.

My object being, first to convince, and then to illustrate by examples, I was obliged to proceed so; and have, therefore, to beg of the reader to be patient, whilst I take him along with me through the thorny road which I have to go, for the purpose of reconnoitering the limits which separate our perishable abode from the everlasting one of the eternal God, and mark the point where man is bound to stop.

A journey through the intricate domains of metaphysics is similar to those scientific or interested expeditions which learned men or traders undertake across the dreary solitudes which are scattered, here and there, over our globe. They advance, accompanied by uneasiness and fatigue; they incessantly look towards the horizon, for the term of their wishes, and never rejoice fully, but when they touch it, unless some unthought-of oasis presents them, from time to time, with a pleasing miniature of the grand and rich treasures after which they pant.

Be, then, still shut to our eyes, ye horrible gates behind which lie the dungeons of death, the iron shackles and chains of human justice, the bloody instruments of public executioners, the exhausted and livid frames of guilty men! Before we come to see the image of God, a prey to the hideous tortures of an unnatural death and to the disgusting inventions of criminal law, feeding public curiosity, hanging lifeless in the middle of a stupid multitude, or launched into eternity from within the walls of a prison, where the secrecy of his punishment bespeaks the ignominy of the law:—we have to enter the silent retreats where cold-blooded men study and write in favour of capital punishment; and those legislative assemblies where Thought, guilty parent of such a cruelty, shows itself with all that which is reprehensible or honourable, wise or unjust in it; and may be yet taught a better lesson, inspired with milder feelings, and abandoned altogether, when legislators understand how impious, how illegal it is.

CAPITAL PUNISHMENT.

PART FIRST.

1. All human power comes from God; that which is good results from the right usage of this power; and that which is bad, is but the abuse of it. But, how will man use it rightly? By never extending it, in any time or case, beyond the limits of his nature and destination; because man cannot assume upon himself to occupy the place of God, and usurp his rights, without being guilty of the most reprehensible abuse of the circumscribed authority with which he has been endowed by his Maker. Thus, if God, because he enjoys the undisputed privilege and means of interverting, suspending, changing the laws which he has established for the safe-keeping of the physical and moral creation, has, in some instances, used, and may still use, that privilege; that proves not that man can do the same, and build upon such exceptions, social institutions. Philosophers and divines of all ages have understood this fundamental principle of every earthly government so well, that they did, at all times, endeavour, the former, to keep man within the narrow compass of our kind, whenever they had to determine his rights, or make him enter into a social compact; and the latter, never to propose him any dogma or mystery to believe, without imposing, I dare to say, upon him this well-known and universal axiom: *God said so.*

2. Indeed, as long as divines, whether pagan or Christian, stand within the creed from which their respective powers emanate, society cannot blame them for saying so; for, in the name of whom might she do it? In the name of God? But, divines in-

voke that sacred name also; and they are not, I think, less worthy of being believed and trusted than any other man or body of men. Then, unless God pleases to become a judge between society and priests, the liberty of thought and speech remains to both, and protects them equally.

3. But if religion is freed from every civil bondage, society also must be freed from every religious fetter. The idea that, in the actual condition of things among us, religion has become the soul of society; that, either directly or indirectly, it will always mix with the social thought which brings forth political pacts, is a mere sophism. It is no more asked whether the Church shall govern the State; whether, in spite of each individual conviction or belief, the Jewish, Pagan, or Christian theocracy shall have power over a civilized nation; but whether men, who now understand mankind and revere God duly, shall dispense with using theocratical notions, when they contribute to frame the constitution of a society in which, for the reciprocal benefit of all, every citizen must be permitted to pray as he pleases.

4. This, I say, is the question. It has been solved long ago, and affirmatively, by the wise of all nations. Hence this sacred motto added to the device of unfettered societies: *The State depends upon God only!* Agreeably to it, neither the religious code of one sect, nor the belief of another, is therein consulted, previously to the enactment of the constitutional law; and that this plan of legislation is, by all means, the best which can be devised, every one will admit who takes notice of this well known fact, that the creed which the followers of Christ think themselves in duty bound to obey, is nothing but an untruth for the Jew, who claims the privilege of keeping undisturbed the law of Moses. As both the Christian and the Jew are an integrant part of the state, belong to it, owe themselves to it, it is evident that the state, which cannot be Christian and Jew at the same time, must, in any order which

it intimates to both, ask the advice of the law of nature, which is obligatory upon both at all times.

5. Some scrupulous minds may rise thereupon, and demand whether I mean that the State shall be atheist? I answer, though it professes no particular religion, the State is not forced, thereby, into atheism: for, what is religion? A mere combination of doctrines and practices established upon a certain belief which varies with each sect. Shall, then, the State be condemned either to embrace the tenets of one sect in preference to the creed of another, or to become atheistical, because it is in favour of neither of them? No. There is a rational medium between the non-admission of a religion and the negation of God. Which is it? God himself. The State will not deny, but imitate him; and, whereas each sect makes God speak so as to find in his words a demonstration of its tenets, start from this capital truth, that, being unable to be wiser than God, it must rule its subjects, as he governs the world; that is to say, without meddling practically with that which belongs to worship. Take out this sound principle, and there cannot be any free society, but tyranny and destruction of all human rights! Take it out, and man will exact from man that which God does not: for God says to man: *Thou mayest believe or not believe, since thou wast made free:* and man says to his like: *I command, Thou shalt believe.* Thus, God is made man, and man is made God. Is that just? Is that rational? No.

6. Every man educated in a particular creed, is unquestionably bound to study and follow it, if he thinks it good, or may change it, if he judges that it is wrong. But, this obligation of man, is evidently an individual one, which, of course, cannot weigh upon society at large. Man is an abstract being, who, first of all, looks to himself, whilst society is a complex one, which belongs to all. Man lives but for himself, in himself, but society has no existence except that of its members taken collectively;

it is the god of earth, so far as it is the principle of every law and of every order which may be enacted thereon; but, at the same time, a god very weak and limited indeed; a god who has to end sooner or later, because he has begun; a god who, as he cannot give life, cannot either inflict death; a god who judges, sees, hears not, but through others, and, therefore must obey, but not master the human intellect upon the whims or good sense of which he altogether depends. He should, certainly, enjoy a perfect freedom within his dominions, but never be allowed to go beyond them, for he would soon usurp a power which he should not have, and render himself so much more dangerous as he would be actuated by the most heterogeneous passions.

7. This principle which every one admits, leads to another, viz. that the arguments drawn from Revelation in favour of a theocracy should not be listened to by legislators. If our Maker had wanted to have the universe governed by his word, either written or spoken, he would have had a care, not only to make the whole world acquainted with it, but also to make every man willing to obey it. Did he do so? no: but, on the contrary, decided that there should be among men, a living principle of liberty, nay, of opposition. Whether enlightened by the evangelical truth or taught by his natural sense, man feels and knows that he is a free agent in matters of religion. Would it not be, then, an absurd usurpation of power, if we wanted him to be governed by authorities and laws which he may either admit or reject, until he settles his accounts with God in the world to come? When our forefathers entered into a society, they could not prevent securing the right of change for their posterity, and respecting that spirit of liberty which presides over every political revolution as it causes every religious reformation. By imitating their example, we make no concession, but comply with an indispensable duty.

8. To be, is the essential attribute of God; and to

pass away, the necessary fate of society. Therefore, to associate revelation with a government is to make it perishable, so far, at least, as it depends upon man; unless one says that, in consequence of such an association, the state is for ever secured, and cannot fail. But this supposition is not borne out by history. No where has revelation, in any shape or manner, saved the world from revolutions. To operate and keep up a wonder of this sort, God should interfere actually with the social progress, have a temple of his own, utter his oracles in it every day, force the accomplishment of his views by gathering all the human family within the same church, and regulating its civil administration. He does not do it! Then practice agrees with theory, to have revelation separated from politics.

9. Divines of modern ages are so well aware that this mode of arguing the question is correct, that they have undertaken to prove by ratiocinations *a contingente* that God has not only spoken, but also left his living word among us; so that it depends only upon men to let this word of God have every where, its full scope. God spoke! Well and good. And that is enough, do you say? Well and good again. But, why is it not enough in fact? Why, in spite of this heavenly intercourse, do we still see Bramins, Mandarines, Turkish priests, Protestant ministers, Jewish rabines, Catholic bishops, who cannot agree? Why do we still see the East Indians laughing at Chinese, Chinese censuring Musulmans, Heretics mocking Catholics, Catholics condemning Heretics, and Jews who flatter themselves of being better informed than the rest of mankind? Why do we still see nations which never understood, and never will, most likely, understand each other? Why? Because God sent on earth, from the beginning, the spirit of freedom, and would destroy the most perfect work of his hands, *Man*, if he had chained thus our kind under the yoke of Theocracy.

10. Any thing that is should be as it is. Let God

be in heaven, and let man remain on earth! We have to render in our hearts to our Maker such a worship as we think we owe him; but we cannot lower him to us, by associating his eternal majesty with the perishable ones which we constitute to suit our convenience or fancy. The Church is not the State; the State is not the Church. Priests may preach, but lawgivers must rule. Morality, like Physics, rests upon secrets which are out of our reach. We know enough of both to be bettered by the one, and helped along by the other, but the mysteries of both are in the hands of God who keeps them for himself, and who, whilst he allowed us to investigate them, ordered us never to mimic or try to equal him.

11. Priests, armed with a mysterious book, are, by no means, more powerful than Genius catching hold of the elements to interrogate them. The universe, according to what our Bible says, is in the hands of man: *Tradidit mundum disputationibus eorum:* and man, consequently, made, as he is, a king of this world, can search it out in every sense, provided he consents to stop, in due time, before the impenetrable veil of the dazzling glory which surrounds the supreme and omnipotent Author of things. The most pious opposition, on the part of Theocracy, cannot impair this right, nor overrule a scientific conclusion for the sake of a long believed religious doctrine. Thus, the Copernican theory was good, in spite of the decision brought against it by the Church of that time; and earth did not stand motionless upon the central point of our solar system, but continued moving around its sun, according to Galileo's doctrine, though ignorant pontiffs and divines condemned that great man, and kept him in a dungeon.

12. But if Theocracy may be mistaken in Physics, it may be so likewise in morals. A Chinese, I am inclined to believe, can be a good and faithful disciple of Confucius, and yet dispense with having his head shaved through a motive of religion; a Turk admit all the doctrines of Mahomet, and yet drink

wine occasionally; a Jew believe sincerely in the various tenets of Moses, and yet help himself, from time to time, to some good oysters; a Christian profess the principles of any Protestant reformation, and yet pass not the whole Sunday in pious reading; a Catholic follow the Church of Rome honestly, and yet doubt the infallibility of the Pope. Cease, then, ye, who command others, to argue in this way. *So the Bible reads! So the Church says!* The Bible and the Church have nothing to do with a political convention or contract. Every legislator may read the one, and obey the other at home, but must leave both there, when he goes to meet with his fellow citizens, for the general welfare of the community to which he belongs. The code of nature is, then, the only one to be consulted by him, because it is common to all and read by all in the same manner. The gospel of Christ agrees upon this principle of legislation with natural philosophy: *Et erat lux vera quae illuminat omnem hominem venientem in hunc mundum.*

13. In as much as it is practised by the generality of a nation, religion is felt more or less in its administration. That is true: nay, it is almost impossible that, accordingly, the national belief of a people be altogether isolated from its civil morals. Political and religious action is one, indeed, when duly understood and properly determined. Hence that spirit of civil forbearance in matters of belief, upon which governments truly liberal seem to rest; they tolerate all sorts of worship, ever since they have conceived God who, though he is one in his infinite essence, bears with, nevertheless, all his creatures who are actually at a perpetual variance with respect to their thousand creeds.

14. I will also acknowledge that, Christ having preached the most perfect of all the religions known upon earth, those nations among whom his has prevailed, are better governed than all others who were not favoured with it; and that, among Christian na-

tions, that one is better administered whose tenets approach nearer the perfection taught by our gospel. No study would be more interesting than this for politicians and lawgivers, as the laws enacted either through the influence of the former, or the actual power of the latter, are, undoubtedly, more or less rational and beneficial, according to the comparative state of practical knowledge and of disinterested virtue in which a Christian society may happen to be.

15. But again, the influence of religion upon civil morals should not be mistaken. It helps it along; secures its good effects, protects the law which, though independent of it in its letter, partakes of its spirit in many things, but controls not society. In a word, the law has to decide, punish, and repress according to its paradigm the law of nature; and, religion has to reproach, reform, and console, according to its object, which is to operate inwardly. Should it be otherwise, the iniquitous laws of the Catholic Inquisition, and of the puritanical theocracy, were justifiable, as they had been made the laws of the land, and these enacted in accordance with the principle of that religious despotism which men are now endeavouring to overthrow.

16. How can a civil government, of which the constitution was framed upon its religious belief, refuse to listen to this religion, when it calls for its assistance? In any place where religion is invoked by the law as a justification of its severity, religion is allowed to borrow from the law its executioners, when it has to punish the infractors of the religious tenets of the land. So did it happen in Athens, when Socrates was condemned to finish his life by poison; and in Jerusalem, when Christ fell a victim to the hatred of the Jews.

17. Unhappily, men inclined to fanaticism are to be met with every where. Therefore, when a civil code reads thus: in the name of God who protects society, and of men who are bound to watch over it in compliance with the divine law; theft, murder,

fraud, fornication, counterfeiting, adultery, felonies of all sorts, shall be punished, these with death, and those with imprisonment; religion will come forth and say: Heresy is worse than theft and murder; the latter attacks the life or the property only of an individual, whilst the former overturns society itself, and throws it into the most dangerous convulsions: punish it, then, with a still greater severity than you would punish theft and murder. That man who purposes to mimick, soil, and destroy your belief, is more criminal than a profligate whose object is to kill, steal, or seduce; for, however guilty may this one be found by you, he never goes out of the narrow circle of individuality, whilst the impious wretch of whom I speak, stretches his assassinating arms all over the globe, and further yet if he could. Let, then, the axe of death with which you sever murderers from life, strike mercilessly all those who kill me in the hearts of men, as I am better than a man, and my death is a greater evil for society than that of an isolated being. So did reason, in former ages, pagan and Christian persecutors; and their mode of arguing, let us confess it, cannot be refuted consistently by any one who thinks that the religious idea of a nation must rule its civil, and, more especially, its criminal laws.

18. It recalls to my remembrance a conversation which I held, several years ago, with a dignitary of the Catholic Inquisition. The reader, I hope, will consider it as an interesting digression.

That man whose eccentric name* agreed, in every way, with his private habits, was introduced to me by a gentleman† whose piety was proverbial in his own country, and had been exiled with him for the same political motives. Astonished, and glad at the same time, to meet with such a personage, I examined him attentively from head to foot, with that feeling of curiosity which is natural to man, when an extraordinary accident throws in his way one of those

* Monte Agudo. † Juan de Navarrette.

prodigious monuments "of decayed greatness" which revolutions leave behind them. He was of a tall and noble looking stature: his pale complexion, white hair thinly scattered over his classical head, calm but intelligent and piercing eyes, prudent smile, accomplished, though perfectly cold, politeness, brief and sententious phraseology, almost inspired look, grave and studied countenance, revealed, at once, what his life had been, what his thoughts were. Austerity and experience, solemn companions of those contemplative minds which have long travelled through regions unknown to other men, a deep knowledge of good and evil, the proverbial prudence of the serpent, and the persuasive simplicity of the dove, that inwardly felt despair of a fallen greatness and anxious mistrust which proceeds from dissipated illusions, the dying smile of a doomed theological absolutism, together with the everliving enthusiasm of mysticism, the sublime, heartfelt resignation of a Christian ambition, conquered at last by philosophy, seemed to have convened for the singular and rare purpose of characterizing in that one man the powerless though for ever stupendous remains of an authority once so formidable. I thought I saw it such as it was when the Pope, a skilful politician, threw it across the path of another prodigy no less remarkable, the immortal Luther!

19. His hand, meanwhile, reposed cold and motionless upon mine, still trembling with that nervous susceptibility which a strong mental agitation creates in the system. Here, then, said I to myself, I have a real genuine fragment of that so far dreaded and now destroyed Inquisition? Its palaces belong to its conquerors. They live and move with a perfect freedom, within those walls which, for so many years, never echoed but the sighs of fear and misery. Its prisons receive, at this time, no other guests except those whom the criminal law of the land immures justly within their horrible dungeons. Crime alone suffers where virtue was so often persecuted.

Its instruments of torture lie there, in some remote room, like mere monuments of curiosity, stained with blood, hierogliphical souvenirs of many devouring griefs. Its ministers, for ever dispossessed, wander like strangers among the crowd which their presence used to inspire with fright. Any one can look with impunity at its frame, thus stripped off and debarred of its former prestiges. Its time has passed away. The Inquisition is dead! yes, dead! And of what use should it be now that the doctrines which it attacked are also dying? Ruins fall upon ruins. So was it to be. Let no man speak of them henceforth, but to pity man's frailty, and better himself if he can!

20. Thus, I say, were my sensations and thoughts absorbed upon past evils, whilst I stood by that unknown, exiled priest! No doubt but that he discovered all that which was passing in my mind and heart, for he smiled politely on me, and said with a calm, cooling sound of voice: Well, my son, what is the matter with you? You seem agitated! Is it my presence here, by these many sects which, like our Inquisition, are to perish, which you wonder at? You would be wrong. No power, except that of God who changes not, can last for ever. Men, and any thing which they have or do, must perish sooner or later; great to-day and low to-morrow, they ascend, it seems, but to fall. The Inquisition and the Lutheran Reformation, according to this law of nature, have gone through their time of glory. Free governments begin theirs; but, like the others, they will also come to an end, and sooner, perhaps, than expected. Any how, they cannot last long!

21. They cannot last long, replied I: and how do you know it? My science, answered the priest, is like that of a farmer who says, "Tempests which spread ruin and death over our fields and meadows, last but one hour, and, sometimes, less; then calmness in the skies, serenity in the air, and the uniform course of the four seasons, come back to last for weeks, months, and, often, years." Those revolu-

tions which tend to destroy and level are like tempests, and, like them, are soon over: then, the old order of things reappears and settles anew among men. Look at Rome, that extraordinary model so often alluded to by politicians! She finished as she had begun, under the sceptre of a crowned head. Republican governments are what we may call the *Mezzo termino* of nations, or, in other words, their epoch of probation, their era of dotage. As soon as, that revolutionary tendency which storms societies has ceased, and when those majestic claps of political thunder, those brilliant flashes of philosophical lightning have done raging, nations will rise silently over the heaps of ruins which so great changes will throw the one over the other, and begin again building their houses where and in the way they stood before, because nations, as well as individuals, are not happy, except at their fathers' homes.

22. I said: This, my father, is a comparison truly beautiful, and, perhaps, exact at the same time; for who knows what is coming; but, what do you see beyond the term of our republican and constitutional governments? What do I see?—nothing, save that which every man who is wise can see, when he studies attentively the history of our kind—nothing, save that which every good and well informed Christian can see, who peruses impartially the annals of our religion; that is to say, an end and a beginning perfectly similar. Man, who came from God without knowing how, goes back to God in the same way. His birth and death are both an act of despotism over which he can have no control whatever. He enters life and leaves it in consequence of a kingly order, though his existence is a sort of a republic, a true exemplification of what we have termed, constitutional freedom. So is it with every civil or religious government. God made them monarchichal; ill-understood liberty brought them both into a republican form; but both have, no matter how

and when, to go back and resume their former condition, which is, if you please, civil and religious catholicism or unity.

23. Then, respected father, added I, you believe that the world shall again be governed by absolute monarchs? Yes. And why? Because our Christian religion, upon which governments of all forms have to depend, shall again be what it was after the downfall of the first heresies, truly catholic, and thereby cause the unity of power to prevail among nations, as it will in the Church. Then, the Church and the State shall be one, as they were before; there shall be but one Master, as there is but one God. No doubt, that in these coming times, both the Church and the State shall have foes to resist, because the race of civil and religious reformers will last as long as the world does; but in any place where peace will be preferred to war, and the untimely death of a few to the general overthrow of society, there will be established, by both powers, two tribunals of inquest; the one for the support of the civil order, the other to protect the national belief. In another and more special phrase, there will be an Inquisition.

24. An Inquisition! exclaimed I; that is impossible, reverend sir: it would be a new crime imagined to punish inoffensive follies. Jesus, the mild, harmless Jesus, has no need of executioners to triumph over the hearts of men. I always blamed Luther for many things, and Paul the Fifth still more. I do hate equally those stupid agents of cruelty, whom our fathers have seen both in Spain and England, obeying the ferocious orders of the Inquisitors and of Elizabeth. I curse the memory of the bloody authors of the Saint Bartholomew's massacres in France; and I will never believe that such atrocities as were perpetrated by them can be consented to by heaven. Nay, my father; should God approve of such a barbarous system of government, I would

instantly deny him. For his sake, speak not as you do!

25. Young man, rejoined calmly the old clergyman, I beg of you to be still; you know not what you say! Listen to me quietly, and you will not, I dare say, be so hasty in your conclusions. What do you know of life? Almost nothing, except that it promises you many pleasures which you shall never enjoy, and threatens you with a few troubles which you will meet with undoubtedly. That which you think to be wrong, may be right; and, reciprocally, that which appears right to you, may be wrong, indeed. You want to do altogether away with the Inquisition: then, the Inquisition is, in your opinion, an institution altogether dangerous; but others, and most especially society, think otherwise. Please to look carefully all around you! At almost every step which you take in the streets, you meet with bailiffs, constables, men-of-arms, justices of the peace, civil and criminal judges. Well! do you know who all those men are? Nothing more nor less than inquisitors, as all our courts of justice are as many inquisitions. Without them, society cannot live; they watch over its morals and the regular keeping of its various laws. What would become of us if their only functions were to stop thieves and murderers? Fornication and adultery, which need and seek darkness, would take place in full day; disorderly men would do according to their own will and passions, without regard or restraint. Fraud and debauchery would, like kingly mistresses, reign scandalously over our cities and villages; public entertainments would be changed into shameful carnivals: in a word, the morals of society would perish miserably amidst a thousand infamies.

26. Thus, by appointing officers whose duty it is to keep a close and watchful eye over what we call public manners; establishing tribunals before which every infractor, and even scandalous contemner of

those manners are amenable; opening prisons in which such as are found guilty of any infraction or contempt of the moral law are kept in durance vile, far from their fellow beings; ordering punishments which are in a proportion to the crimes; society complies, methinks, with a sacred obligation. But by so doing, does it not also sanction this very principle of the Inquisition which you reprove, and admit practically that it is good in itself? yes certainly.—Then, the Inquisition is not reprehensible, like any other institution, but on account of such abuses as it has been guilty of.

27. I am friend enough of truth, which I do always invoke as a guide in any thing which I undertake to do, to acknowledge sincerely that many culpable usurpations took place in those ecclesiastical tribunals which are now destroyed; that, many a time, cruelty assumed there the cloak of justice to conceal its criminal designs and deeds; that, oftener yet, inquisitors confounded human weakness with depravity, and condemned innocence to chastisements and sufferings which were intended for guilt only. All that I must and do acknowledge willingly. I am sorry for it. I deplore it more still than you do, my dear friend, because I have been an inquisitor, and feel that the wrongs of the Inquisition fall, partly, back upon me. But, tell me, you who speak of horrors, infamies, and crimes, when the Inquisition turns to be the subject of your conversations; have you ever, like Cleophas, with the devil on two sticks, travelled through our courts, palaces, gambling houses, brothels, hospitals, prisons, exchanges, markets, theatres, and other secret and public places? I believe you have not. Do, then, at once: and, when your journey is over, come back here to tell me candidly where do all those horrors, infamies and crimes which our kind is capable of, actually take place?

28. Perhaps, you will say to that, that the wrongs of some men are not an excuse for justice, which, as

it is established to redress wrongs and punish guilt, is, of course, bound to avoid both. I agree with you here, but you must agree with me, that justice, however honourable, as it should be, has often been, and often is, in the hands of men, a means of depravity for some, and an occasion of abuse for many. For example: what do you think of those laws which, though they cannot reach but ostensible facts, give up the conscience of a man to another, and make this one an absolute judge of it? What do you think of those laws which strike at random, and inflict the same blow both on the ignorant and the wise; weigh equally upon the strong and the weak; order the same punishments for the unfortunate, who prevaricates through a sort of necessity which poverty causes, and the shameless villain, who commits crime to satisfy his perverted appetites? What do you think of those laws which mix together corruption which begins, with consummated roguery, or, for the purpose of avoiding such a mixture, isolate, for years, one man from his like, set him face to face with a jailer, whose look inspires mistrust and fear, with a sort of heartless creature whom they call turnkey, and tell him, through an iron wicket, *thinkest thou, depraved man, thinkest thou!* What do you think of those laws which command that a prisoner must, no matter what the comparative guilt of his conscience is, atone, between four walls, and amidst the painful toils of a trapist, for the theft of a few yards of cloth, of a barrel of flour, of a small sum of money; whilst the most formidable robber is allowed to sleep upon a bed as good as his, in the next cell, share with him the same pittance, enjoy, if I dare say so, the same sufferings with him? Had the Inquisition invented those laws and inconceivable systems of correction, men should cry out, scandal! scandal! A quorum of free-thinkers have imagined them, and fools consider them as a wonderful discovery! So goes the world, my dear friend.

29. Some philosophers pretend that a man, who

is tired of living in society which he has either scandalized, or has to complain of, and whose conscience is his better judge, should not be allowed to inflict upon himself the penalty of retiring into a lonesome convent, put on the monastic cowl, exercise his mind amidst pious sorrows, and chastise his body with a hopeful severity; and, for a petty offence, which is hardly punishable in the eyes of God, they want to impose on another such tribulations, as would be considered most hard and unbearable in the severest monastery, without permitting him, in the meantime, to enjoy what the most austere rules of any religious order will guarantee. I mean the unalienable right of disclosing one's conscience to whom one pleases. Is there not a striking similarity between this sort of justice and that of some religious reformers, who impose upon their disciples all the privations ordered by the Church of Rome to its subjects, and refuse them all the enjoyments which the latter permits? When some of our prison reformists say: I isolate a man for a theft, but let him free though he speaks blasphemy; methinks I hear a dissenter proclaim: Believe not in the real presence of our Lord in the Eucharist, it is a dangerous absurdity, but forget not to read the Bible, it is the foundation of all!

30. This I say, continued the priest, not to censure men, but to acquaint you with the world. In it, my son, every thing is right or wrong, according to the view which this present age takes of the one or the other system which may be proposed. For example, look now at our institution of a jury? Many philosophers blame it, whilst it is approved by many others who maintain that no better means of administering justice could be contrived. As this last opinion prevailed, a jury must be empanelled for every case whether civil or criminal. Twelve men often unacquainted with the law of the land, and ready rather to obey the instinctive impulse of their

heart or mind, than the proofs which result from testimony, take coldly their seats opposite to a fellow being who, for the most part, understands nothing of what is going on, except that two other men, the one employed by him, and the other by the State, try their best, the former to save him from death or prison, the latter to secure either his life for the hangman, or his body for a jailor, and both to prevail, no matter how, upon the minds of the jurors whose obligation it is to stand there, until the one has exhausted his science to soothe, and the other used all his eloquence to excite them. Answer me candidly. Is such a system so very admirable? No, father! said I, it is not.

31. However, resumed he, it is now more than ever abided by; those struggles between life and death, prison and liberty, which our laws allow, must ultimately enlighten the conscience of a jury, and make them decide upon the fate of the accused. In virtue of this principle, which for many, is truly a scandal, society hangs a man, without feeling any remorse for such a deed which you condemn; the accuser sleeps more calmly; the judge eats his dinner more comfortably: the conscience of the jury is alleviated; and the trade of both the sheriff and the executioner made perfectly honourable. What do you think of men?

32. I think, sir, that they are much to be pitied. That which you have just said, is but the expression of a frightful truth; and such is my conviction with respect to this dangerous mode of rendering justice to criminals, that I have long desired to have a favourable opportunity to attack it, by writing both against capital punishment and the partial mysticism which seems to have prevailed in some prisons, that I might contribute to the total abolition of the former, and to the salutary reformation of the latter. But you, my father! who have so well understood the errors of mankind on this subject, and criticised them so eloquently, how can you defend the laws, neither

less barbarous, nor less absurd of the Catholic Inquisition?

33. The old man smiled keenly, and said: I apprehend you have misunderstood me. It was my intention neither to blame nor to approve that which you are pleased to call *the errors of mankind;* but to establish a mere comparison between the social and the religious justice in criminal matters. Society may inflict upon malefactors of all sorts such punishments as suit it best. In whatsoever manner it punishes crimes, it will err most assuredly, because the conscience of man is and will always be a mystery for his like, who, for this reason, will never be able to act upon it with any certainty. Now, as it cannot be otherwise, and as, on the other hand, crimes must be punished, you see that this error of society is excusable. But, if we excuse society with respect to its faults and cruelties in matters of criminal justice, methinks that the Inquisition might be excused too, notwithstanding the mistakes it may have made in matters of heresies and religious scandals, and the barbarous executions which some of the inquisitors have been culpable of.

34. I will grant it. In the present state of things, men run often the chance of mistaking one end for another, and may make a bad use of that which is right and good in itself. Perhaps you are neither more liberal or more indulgent than I am with regard to this? Thus, you find fault with the mysticism which prevails in certain prisons, and I like it; you consider capital punishment as a judicial murder, and I do not: solitary cells, in which robbers may repent whilst they suffer, and the gallows upon which murder is repaid with murder, do perfectly agree with my notions of the Inquisition; but yours which are of a nature altogether philosophical, reject these two chastisements of crime. Which of us is in the right? This is a question which never will be definitely solved.

35. With regard to my opinion, I am satisfied

that every man who has had to deal with evil-doers, will admit that it is perfectly rational. Solitary dungeons free our jailers from many clogs; and the gallows is, no doubt, a very conclusive argument. You may laugh at a proof which I draw from my entering into the views and ideas of a turnkey upon this subject, and find it rather extraordinary that a divine will associate with prison-keepers and executioners to get more safely rid of mischievous and sanguinary men; but I have on my side many philosophers, whose reasonings I prefer to yours; so true it is that philsophy does sometimes agree with theology, and may pursue the same object, whilst they seem to be so far from each other, and oppose each other both in their doctrines, and their moral action upon society! . . .

36. And, in order that you may be better able to see how correct I am when I say so, I will compare the regulations of a penitentiary, for example, with those which were followed in the cells of the Catholic Inquisition. In both places, the prisoners, though convicted upon motives and objects very different, seem to have been doomed to an equal fate. There, in penitentiaries, criminal justice isolates thieves, counterfeiters, wretches of all sorts, and tells them: *Work* now, *read* and *think!* for *working* kills the time, *thinking* purifies the mind, and *reading* betters the heart. Here, in the solitary dungeons of the Inquisition, heretics, schismatics, unbelievers were shut up for the peace of the Church and the good of their souls: they were also told to read and think, but not to work; as the inquisitors were convinced that a power which undertakes to restore a man to moral health, should provide also for the entertainment of his body, without exacting any extra charge. They obliged their convicts neither to weave nor to make shoes, nor follow any other trade; and this modification speaks rather in favour of us inquisitors; for it seems to me that covetousness must compete with depravity in those jails

where speculation lends its assistance to justice. But, perhaps I am mistaken; and, consequently, will not insist too much upon our comparative merit.

37. Such an original censure on the part of a priest astonished me. I smiled. He continued: Those philanthropists who are in favour of penitentiaries, say also; by isolating, thus, convicts from each other, circumstantial guilt is kept off from every dangerous contact with inveterate rascality: so that, whilst studied villains are forced to weigh and feel in their consciences all the horror with which their crimes strike society, and perchance, taught to hate them as an evil; inexperienced robbers are helped along in the salutary way of sorrow, during their solitary confinement, and better prepared to obey virtue, when, after a secret penance, they enter the world again. Were I like you, my son, I might comment, much and long, upon these considerations; nay, refute them to your satisfaction: but, inasmuch as they concur with the intended purposes of the Inquisition, I will take them for as many granted arguments. In our prisons, dissenters of every kind were also, and above all, condemned to reflect upon the bad consequences of heresies, schisms and unbelieving philosophy. Each of them, left to himself in a gloomy cell, was thereby enabled to measure, profitably for his soul, the width and depth of the abyss which he had opened with his own hands, and into which he was about to be hurled, when the charitable arm of the Inquisition came to his rescue, and saved him from any further peril, by securing his person between four walls, and devoting him to a beneficent, healing silence.

38. Moreover, we had, like your philanthropists in penitentiaries, a moral means of reform: theirs, is the Bible, such as it has been handed down to us by our ancestors, or rather priests. They take that book, present it to the prisoner, and tell him: *Read*, and you will *repent: read*, and you will *improve in virtue: read*, and you will *turn an honest man.*

Ours, methinks, was a still better one; for, it was not to a book; but to a man that we left the charge of operating, with some advantage, upon the mind and heart of a fellow being. That man used to say, "Hark, you unfortunate sinner! and listen to me: the Church, our Holy Mother, orders you to believe what she teaches us. Listen, and you will understand; listen, and you will be convinced; listen, and you will submit." Certainly, good sense shows that; with respect to this point, inquisitors were more consistent with themselves than philanthropists are; for, what may be, upon the mind of a man reproved either by society or by religion, the power of a book which, (as it has no authority but through that of an interpreter, who, by-the-by, should be the primitive or Roman Catholic Church,) yields, naturally, wherever religious liberty prevails, to any commentary which every reader is willing to make upon its texts, and supplies, in some manner, every wrong with a plausible excuse; whereas we find that murder is legalized and falsehood sanctioned in it.

39. The Inquisition, as it was fully aware of this mysterious fact, invoked an authority by far superior; I mean human testimony, which is kept alive in the archives and infallible doctrines of the church. It spoke to a man the language of man; placed him face to face with the imposing monument of a church which cannot err; and never uttered but these indisputable sentences: *The Church is right: you are wrong.* And if some one would pretend to say here, that this mode of proceeding was arbitrary; I will answer, that every law, whether civil or criminal, proceeds thus, by *yes* and *no*. Any where the Inquisition shall prevail, society will know, to a certainty, what it must believe and do; whilst, if the Bible alone guides its operations and progress, there will not be a safe rule of government for it; as one may deserve to be burnt alive and damned to-morrow, on account of his belief in the very same tenets which seem to raise him, to-day,

above others, and secure his admission into heaven. Young man, what do you say to that?

40. I say, father, that you are a good logician; your reasonings are clear, easy, solid—nay, peremptory, if your principles might be admitted; but they are wrong, very wrong; I blame, in many things, penitentiaries, though not for the same motives which cause me to hate the Inquisition. Whatever argument you may bring in favour of them, to justify your own course, I cannot help stating that this mode of chastisement in society is nothing but a reprehensible application of a religious severity imagined by men to excuse social idleness. The conversion of a rogue to virtue in a state prison is no more possible, I think, than the forced repentance of an unbeliever in a dungeon. Open his dungeon, and the man, who, after a long, painful imprisonment, promised to respect the tenets for the violation of which he was shut up by the priests, will not hesitate to attack them again, and try to defeat them if he can. So is it with a convict truly criminal! free him once, and you will see him go back again to his former habit, depravity! Such is the nature of man, that, whereas his guilt is the fruit of his liberty, he cannot turn really better, but when he enjoys it. If necessity weighs upon him, and grief is wrought in him by it, he will become a hypocrite to escape both necessity and grief; but virtue, pure, genuine virtue shall, by no means, be a part of his calculations. Priests and philanthropists cannot, with respect to this tendency to infidelity or vice, be either wiser or more powerful than God; and the examples drawn from some convicts who were converted to virtue in their cells, speak rather against than in favour of penitentiaries; for, either morality can do something in a prisoner's mind, or is of no use to him. In the first case, he is bettered by the laudable exercise of his liberty, and, therefore, should be allowed to enjoy it anew; whilst, in the second case, society, in spite of all its philosophy, will only

have another villain to dread, as soon as its pretended convert comes out from prison.

41. Well, my son, exclaimed the inquisitor, I see you are consistent with yourself. Penitentiaries do, in your opinion, resemble the Inquisition: therefore, both are equally condemned by you, and, should it depend upon you, both would be rejected by society. I admire and praise your impartiality; but, again—is the question which we have been debating, solved according to your views, because both of these institutions may be justly censured and condemned by many?—no, indeed. Other men, and I am one of them, do positively adhere to the doctrine which you refuse to believe. If society could subsist without religion, I would, here in your presence, take in my hand the two systems of Penitentiaries and the Inquisition, dash them both at your feet, and trample with you upon them mercilessly; but whereas religion is, notwithstanding every contradictory effort or notion, an essential part of society, there must be penitentiaries or an Inquisition; penitentiaries as long as civil Protestantism prevails, because human justice stands actually in need of a mysticism, no matter what; and an Inquisition, as soon as there shall be but one belief legalized by the State, because the followers of that belief will think themselves in duty bound to frighten and punish its foes.

42. The idea, that the Inquisition is an invention of the Catholic Church, is evidently mere nonsense. If I am not mistaken in my historical recollection, the Inquisition existed among the Greeks, and caused there the untimely death of the virtuous but unbelieving Socrates. It existed throughout the vast dominions of ancient Rome, whose prefects ordered, here and there, in the name of the emperors, to have all the Christians pitilessly butchered for the purpose of destroying Christianity. It existed, according to our gospel, in Judea, whose high priests nailed Jesus Christ upon a cross for having, as they said, violated the law of Moses. Chinese and Japanese have

also their Inquisition, the object of which is to prevent Christians from entering China and Japan, and do away legally with such missionaries who dare to infringe that prohibition. Turks employ it as a means to authorize Christian slavery among them. Protestant reformation has sanctioned and used it, in Geneva under Calvin; in England under Henry VIII., who killed his wives; Queen Elizabeth, who beheaded her lovers; Cromwell, who murdered his king; in America, among certain pilgrims who cut off the ears of several Quakers, through respect for a religion which these last believed not. History, my son, keeps all those events and many others of the same kind, recorded for the instruction of the wise. But, quote history now-a-days, and you will see the lips of men parting, their eyes wondering at what you say, and their minds very nearly impressed with doubt!

43. Father, replied I, do you indeed approve of all those horrid and sanguinary actions? This is, answered the priest, a question which should not be put to me alone, but also to lawgivers of all countries. All that which I can say is, that times make men and men times. As long as a society thinks that it cannot get rid of an enemy, but by punishing him with death, it can do it and be excused. And should any one say that this is a jesuitical answer, I will reply that, in this case, almost the whole world has adopted the principles of Ignatius and his disciples; for there are but a very few men who think not as I do. The one kills to content his deceived love: the other to defend his political opinion; many to support either their passions or belief. No matter what the object of a murder may be! I look only at the intention of the murderer. It is to infliet death; then why could not society do what a man does, and retaliate?

44. Mighty God! I exclaimed, behold one of thy priests, and he sanctions judicial murders! Why not! murmured, with a lower and still more solemn tone of voice, the grave inquisitor; there is no mur-

der, sir, but where and when society proclaims that there is. So there was a time in which society supported religion, and authorised it to erect ecclesiastical tribunals, before which heretics were amenable, and could be put to death like as many criminals. Now, religion is almost left alone, and can no more punish its foes; but society enforces still in its favour the right of killing, which it denies to religion. We have nothing to say. As long as the world goes so, you may be an unbeliever, impious, protest as much as you please in matters of faith, you run no danger; but if you violate the law of the land by shedding blood, your days are numbered: you must give blood for blood, and die. What is, was to be. Let us no more reason about it!

45. These were his last words: then, turning around, he directed his steps towards a small altar which he had in his bedroom. My eyes rested attentively upon him; he knelt before an image of Christ, the saddest proof of all that is iniquitous in the right which men assumed to punish with death. He prayed, calmly and fervently, for a little while; rose silently, put on his priestly attire, and offered up to God the blood of Jesus his Saviour, with a piety not less wonderful than his doctrine. More than an hour elapsed, before he seemed to think again of this world; what a man!

46. And now, reader, what are we to think of him? He was well informed in many things, and as sincere as one can be who intends to be virtuous; he did not like to scrutinize things beyond their apparent depth; he would take them as they stood before him, look at them coldly, and satisfy himself with saying: That may not be right, but so it is. Then he used to act always in a perfect accordance with contingencies. A striking type of religious mysticism and political craft, he was inclined to judge of human events and revolutions like a blind man, and speak as if he had been deaf to every reasoning which seemed to him conducive to a reformation.

Many other individuals, no doubt, think, feel, see and act as he did; but this fact is, happily, no real obstacle to the progress of mankind.

47. Meanwhile I stood astonished and motionless by him, many sad thoughts were preying upon my mind. I saw clearly that self interest had led his intellect astray, and that he had defended so warmly the errors of our civil legislations about capital punishment, only because the Inquisition had, at one time, set to the world a bad example, which he thought it was his duty to justify. The study of a divinity founded upon a religious absolutism, had misguided within him the wholesome perceptions of a wise philosophy. The secret of his strange doctrines was the fear he had to expose his religion, by confessing that its interpreters had been wrong, and that the unnatural severity of our criminal codes was nothing else but a scandalous relic of a barbarous theocracy.

48. Was he right in obeying such a sentiment? I believe he was not. Religion, I mean the true one, cannot vary. It will stand for ever, pure, undefiled, unimpaired; but priests may err. Like God, its eternal and infallible author, religion can bear every investigation; but priests, who are men, and therefore liable to many dangerous passions, may have their motives not to allow their fellow beings a close investigation of their acts.—So did I reason with myself; and, finding that my mind was labouring under no illusion whatever, I let the inquisitor disappear: I raised my hands to heaven, and uttered behind the man, who, like the power which he had enjoyed, was but an image of vanity, this short but heartfelt sentence: No, it is not so! God and religion enter for nothing in the enactment of a criminal code. I can, I will demonstrate that it is so!—let the reader decide whether I have accomplished my design!

49. However cruel and lamentable may be the fate of a human being, given up by the law to such punishments as are inflicted in our prisons, in the

name of society, there is yet a remedy left. At any time an act of judicial barbarity or injustice is made known, and in proportion as a better understood philanthropy will prevail among men, better days may shine over an innocent, or the pains of a prison alleviated in favour of repenting guilt. But, pray, what consolation has society placed by a scaffold? What remedy has it prepared by the grave which contains the bodies of those whom it has either hanged or beheaded?

50. God, will you say, God!—But since when has man inherited the right of assigning the place on which his Maker must stand, and the time within which he must operate? When has heaven been left to the disposal of earth? Shall repentance enter a guilty conscience, when a perishable sinning judge will think proper to hand over to an executioner, the body in which that conscience dwells?—From the time in which legislators decide that it is so, and dare to command God, there will be no folly which cannot be legalized; no crime which cannot be sanctioned; no horror which cannot be perpetrated with impunity by society!

51. In order that society might kill judicially, its legislators should have received a special inspiration from God to this purpose. The life of man is not like his property. The latter is evidently the original object of a social contract, or a consequence of legislative combinations; whilst the former is a grant from God alone. Therefore, earth, its products whether natural or resulting from some human industry, belong to man, who can do with them what he pleases; but man himself belongs exclusively to God; and what belongs thus to God cannot be alienated in any way, without the special consent of God. This is not a mere proposition, but a standing axiom!

52. Let us understand well its main consequences! As soon as men meet together to form a society; they have a right to compromise about property, and determine by the law, any coincidence or case which

relates to it. Hence our laws upon contracts, wills, marriages, taxes, political constitutions, which allow us to sell, bargain, barter what we have, and pass it to any person whom we are pleased to prefer, and with whom we can deal, either upon a promise, a condition, or a simple acceptance! hence, also, the power which we have to engage our services, enlist ourselves, take arms for the common defence of society, renounce our liberty for a given time, trust our rights to legal protectors, abandon our wrongs to authorized redressers or controllers; in a word, to submit to a legislation, the duty of which it shall be to lay down clear and positive rules, with regard to a good civil and criminal administration!

53. But, in no instance can we dispose of our lives, without infringing a law of nature. The necessity in which we may happen to be of exposing them, in complying with another law of the same code, is, as I will prove it soon, no reason why we should arrogate such a power. That which one man cannot do with regard to himself, cannot be done by him, with regard to society. Millions of men assembled together for the purpose of forming a single society of mankind, have no more power than any one of them taken separately: for, the authority granted to rulers by those sorts of universal meetings, derives, necessarily, from the authority which individuals receive from nature.

54. Now, what sort of an authority has man received from nature with regard to his life, but that of exposing it in the case of self-defence? For motives which he was not willing to explain, God has permitted that man is liable to be attacked by some ferocious beasts, among which man does, sometimes, range; and, therefore, allows him to expose his existence, whenever, in consequence of another law, not less mysterious, it is menaced either by a beast or by a man. Or, as his living in society does not free him from such attacks, but on the contrary; it follows from this circumstance, that he can expose

his life for society, when society has to defend itself against an aggressor. Hence wars and single combats!

55. But the right which society has of calling its subjects to arms, to march with them against a common enemy, involves by no means, the power of committing judicial murders upon an isolated being, whose crime never offended but a single individual; for, how would this power be a consequence of the right mentioned above? Because nature seems to tell it! I have already suggested, and will more amply demonstrate in another paragraph of this inquiry, that it is not so. Because our Bible does positively establish it! but we are to understand that the laws published by Moses rule society no more. Indeed, those laws should be sacred for the Jews whom God governed by himself; but we cannot frame the code of modern societies upon a revelation granted to a nation which exists no more.

56. However holy and respectable may the Bible of the Jews be, it should rule no more among Christian nations, at least, with regard to their social contracts and political progress; for the testament which they contain has been annulled long ago; and, if any of the various laws enacted in it, is still obligatory; it is not because that law is a part of the Jewish Bible, but because it is a necessary consequence of the universal legislation of Nature. When Christ expired on the cross, and sealed with his blood the new religious code which it was his intention to make the whole earth legatary of, he accomplished all the prophecies which related to him; freed men from all the tenets published in Israel, from Moses down to his own time; did away with all those ordinances, laws, and regulations which were not less oppressive in their forms than incomprehensible in their spirit; and tore actually into pieces the first covenant, as Paul indicates expressly in his epistle to the Galatians: Thus, there is now no relation whatsoever between the Christian and Jewish faith; the

Christian and the Jew co-use not the same legislation, and the immensity of Christ separates them from each other. For .motives which we should not endeavour to investigate, God judged proper to govern, punish and reward by himself the race of Israel; but Jesus Son of God, and sent on earth by Him for the purpose of reforming mankind, and calling indiscriminately all nations within the same pale, Jesus, I say, has sundered for ever human from divine institutions, earthly from heavenly laws; and through him, God has declared that his kingdom was no more of this world. *Regnum meum non est de hoc mundo.* What has been done is done!

57. We may have a conclusive proof of it, by comparing the acts of the first Christian apostles with those of the Jewish prophets. The latter used to mingle in the political administration of their country, whilst the former did openly avow, every where they went, that they had nothing to do with the law of the land. In Judea, the priests were an essential part of the government; administered justice, ordered executions; nay, took often upon themselves to punish with their own hands, such convicts as had deserved to be severely chastised, and provoked the holy ire of heaven. Among Christians, on the contrary, the clergy professed a blind, respectful, attentive submission to human power; taught the faithful to revere it as a power resulting from the various political combinations of which the law of nature is the primary cause, so far as it secures the freedom of mankind in regard to politics and morals: *quae sunt a deo ordinata sunt;* and maintained, consequently, that any Christian who would resist the established authority, would resist also the laws enacted by the Author of nature from the beginning of things: *qui potestati resistit dei ordinationi resistit.* In a word, they adhered sincerely to this decisive precept of Jesus, "render to .Caesar what belongs to Caesar, and to God what belongs to God," and rather than to depart from such a wise

and holy commandment, they would have suffered, and did, often, suffer death.

58. Then, from the day on which Christ died for mankind, reconciled them with heaven, and set to them the best examples of virtue, Theocracy is reproved. God, satisfied with the principles of sanctification left on earth by Christ, has ceased to govern politically; he has taken back his rights, and never since, that I know of, invested with them any person, priest or layman, prophet, or worker of miracles. Whatever reasoning is brought to impair this truth, it stands undeniable. Thanks to Jesus, his eternal Father reigns but in our minds through faith, and in our hearts through charity. Thanks to the excellent doctrines established in the Christian testament, the power of legislation is recalled to its natural source, human will, the obligation of which it is never to depart from the law of nature. Any man who says it is not, makes a Jew of himself, or rather steals from heaven an authority which, like the sacred fire Prometheus took away, cannot be used on earth, without exposing it to the most dreadful convulsions, and precipitating mankind into every sort of trouble and mischief.

59. This, I say, is a principle from which we have to conclude that whosoever defends theocracy, wages war against God. Thus, the Inquisition was an iniquitous power! its intent was criminal, its action altogether Jewish, and its existence a scandal to the world. Without any mission from above, it took upon itself to judge Christians and heathens, and dared to punish them in the same manner, as certain prophets of Israel did chastise the Bethsamites, as the famous Samuel slew king Agag, a victim of the celestial wrath. This is a historical fact, which leads naturally to the following question: Did not the Inquisition, by such an usurpation of power, endeavour to entangle God in a bloody contest and compromise horribly the sanctity of a religion which, as its divine author says, needs no earthly support?—

Undoubtedly it did. Men, therefore, had a right to accuse the Inquisition, to confront it with civilization, inflict upon its defenders the stigma of barbarity, and overthrow it as soon as happier circumstances made them able to do so.

60. But, if the Inquisition deserved to be cursed by mankind, all those tribunals which were erected for a similar purpose by almost all the protestant sects must be reproved also. No where, and in no time, should the Christian faith depend upon the death of an unbeliever! So, when cruel sectarians ordered instruments of torture, and raised up scaffolds with the guilty intention of sacrificing upon them their adversaries in religion, they insulted God, renewed the horrors invented by the synagogue to torment Christ, dragged him anew, as it were, along their public squares, and nailed him again on the cross, in the person of one of his disciples. Such a legislation was nothing but a flagrant violation and detestable profanation of our gospel, which does positively command Christians never to use any weapons but those of prayer and penance.

61. But, if impiety has ceased to be a just cause of death among Christians, why should murder be so still? If the Mosaic law is abolished, why does civil law among us maintain the exercise of a Jewish severity against murderers? In order that it might be justifiable in so doing, our gospel should have made an exception with regard to capital punishment in certain cases. Is it so? No.—Christ destroyed the Old Testament in an absolute manner. Its code teaches and orders charity only. His will formally expressed is that we should, in no way, and in no instance, arrogate to ourselves such powers as would interfere with those of his heavenly Father; and to confirm what he meant by some solemn examples, he not only asked not for the death of those who killed him, but excused them in his heart, and prayed to Heaven for them.

62. The only word of his which seems, I will not

say, to sanction, but to admit as a legal fact, the existence of capital punishment, is the one which he directed to Peter; when this apostle, indignant at the treason of Judas, and the infamous conduct of the Jews, severed with a blow of his sword the ear of a certain Malchus: "Put up thy sword again into its place, for all they that take the sword shall perish with the sword:"—but this was a mere observation and not a law made by him. He meant only to express what the law was, and not what it should be. As he was, then, a simple subject of Rome, he spoke in presence of the Roman justice, as we would speak in presence of our own: "My friend, kill not, for any one who kills shall be killed."

63. In speaking so, we mean not that our justice is naturally invested with the right of killing; but, simply, that such is the letter or effect of our criminal law. Since it was customary among Romans to punish maiming and murder with death; Christ, whose duty it was, as a citizen, to respect and obey the law of the land, admonished his friend and begged him to mind it. The remarks of the supposed son of Joseph the carpenter, should not be taken as commands intimated by Christ the Son of God. Every Christian, I think, understands this well!

64. If Christ had intended to sanction capital punishment in his evangelical code, he would not have failed to explain clearly his views upon a subject so important, to tell us how and when the law of grace should be amalgamated with our criminal law, and and render our judicial executions justifiable. The subject, I say, was of such consequence as to require that he would enter into the minutest details, and repeat them, for our political information, as often as he did those lessons of which the object was to acquaint us perfectly with the excellent morals which he made a present of to mankind.

65. Consequently, the words mentioned above are, indeed, but an observation relating to the many conjectures which human liberty has changed, through

abuse, into practical facts. But where are the wise who will dare to conclude, from a mere conjecture alluded to by Christ, and respected by him in its civil application, during his mortal career, that society inherited the right of punishing with death? Whenever a doubt arises with regard to a momentous question, which is itself connected with the law of nature, man should endeavour to solve it, not with the subtle ratiocination which qualifies a sophist, but in accordance with the most probable meaning of such authorities as he is inclined to be led by in his investigations and judgments. Let us, then, consult the spirit of Jesus, study his actions, and see whether in his words or examples we can find a rational motive, that we may suppose that there existed in his mind a thought so evidently opposed to the mildness of heart and disposition to forgive which distinguished him.

66. "I will have mercy, and not sacrifice, did he often say: for I am not come to call the righteous, but sinners to repentance.—Go rather to the lost sheep of the house of Israel.—The Son of Man is come to save that which was lost.—A bruised reed shall he not break, and smoking flax shall he not quench, till he send forth judgment unto victory.—I say unto you which hear, Love your enemies; do good to them which hate you.—Be ye, therefore, merciful, as your Father is merciful.—I say unto you, that likewise joy shall be in heaven over one sinner that repenteth, more than over ninety-and-nine just persons which need no repentance.—Thus it is written, and thus it behoved Christ to suffer, and to rise from the dead, the third day; and that repentance and remission of sins should be preached in his name, among all nations, beginning at Jerusalem.—Ye judge after the flesh, I judge no man, judge not according to appearance, but judge righteous judgment.—Ye know not what manner of spirit ye are of; for the Son of Man is not come to destroy men's lives, but to save them.—He that is without sin

among you, let him first cast a stone at her, (the adulterous woman.)—Woman, where are those thine accusers? Has no man condemned thee?—She said, No man, Lord: and Jesus said unto her, Neither do I condemn thee: go, and sin no more."

67. Thus did Christ speak in his time; and his deeds, so are we informed by the sacred writers, agreed admirably with his words: *Caepit Jesus facere et docere!* Now, is it probable, that a religious lawgiver, whose precepts were so exclusively founded upon a true spirit of charity and forgiveness, was willing to sanction the custom of spilling the blood of man legally; of cutting short the way which leads to crime, by severing with an axe the head of a man from his body, or hanging him by the neck? No; his mission was to tell us that, through him, the merciless justice which crushes down guilty men, and punishes them for ever, had been removed to heaven, where it waits until man is dead, to judge him without appeal; but that, upon earth, an ample, nay, unlimited room, has been left for regrets and useful remorse. He intended that man should remain here, face to face, with his own conscience; that, after having had from God the necessary time to know and expiate his faults, he should have, in the life to come, nobody else to accuse but himself. But the measurer of this time is God, not man; let us not forget it!

68. In consequence of this wise regulation of Christ, the distance which exists naturally between God and man has been recognised and re-established. God mixes no more with civil legislation, though he inspires lawgivers with wise ideas, that they may govern rightly; and man exercises no more the rights of God, though he kneels sincerely before his omnipotent majesty. God controls the mind; man controls the external acts. Man may chastise, but God alone inflicts death, as he alone can impart the benefit of life. Prisons, with that appalling accompaniment of troubles, sorrows, humiliations, mental

and bodily sufferings which they comprise, are at the disposal of man: but death!—let us believe it firmly,—death cannot be handled by any earthly power. So, suicides, murderers, judges who condemn a man to die, executioners who kill him, are all guilty of the greatest of all crimes before God, who will reproach and condemn them for having, in the abusive exercise of their liberty, anticipated the time marked by his providence, whose designs they should have respected. Prejudice, perhaps, and social error will be an excuse for executioners and judges; but, like the others, they will have to answer the charge of murder, and invoke for themselves the mercy which they will have refused to others.

69. This, indeed, is a severe remark: but what can we think of a Christian judge who passes coldly sentence of death upon a fellow Christian, and orders him to lower his head under the axe of justice; to give up his throat to the strangling rope of the law? Does he, however learned a judge he may be, know to a certainty what is to become of the victim of his judicial vengeance? No. The fate of a hanged or beheaded criminal is as mysterious for us, as that of a suicide, or of one who has fallen by the hand of an assassin. The only thing we are taught to believe is, that the after-happiness or unhappiness of a man depends altogether upon the comparative state of justice or wickedness of his conscience at the time in which he left this world for ever: but we cannot say what that state was; for we know not the hour in which the grace of God either prevails in the heart of man or abandons it. Then, what does a judge do, who launches fearlessly in those unknown regions of a formidable eternity, a guilty man, whose hour of repentance is not in the power of his executioner? He encroaches upon the will of God. Jesus, the divine interpreter of that secret will, has said that the Spirit of God whispers where and when he pleases; so that no one but God

can regulate it. And a man, because he is a judge, says to that Spirit: Behold! to-morrow we kill a man! Inspire him, if thou pleasest, this evening, or early in the morning, with a thought of regret; for we can wait no longer!

70. That human justice proceeds thus, every one avows. Now, I ask you plainly: Can its conduct be altogether blameless in the eyes of God? do our criminal judges presume that the social error, which they will not fail to allege as a sufficient excuse, grants them the power of precipitating, for a criminal offence, one of their fellow beings into that stupendous abyss of death from which no one can be recalled. Saints and angels themselves cannot either hurry or recall the hour of repentance in the heart of a sinner; it remains in the hands of God alone. So, when a criminal judge takes upon himself to mark it, he arrogates the power of God, opens the gates of hell, and plays with eternity, like a child would with a toy, the mechanism of which is unknown to it. What is he to expect in the life to come?

71. Such reasonings, it is understood, are exclusively directed to believers: being myself fully convinced of the Christian faith, I confess I have often perused them, and did, as many times, shudder with an appalling sensation, when I opposed, in my mind, to the impertinent boldness of our criminal justice, this undeniable truth, that the disposal of the divine grace is out of our reach, and that we can, in no manner, expose our like to the eternal curse of God. So, notwithstanding any argument on the part of those who would contradict me, I cannot see, in the person of a judge who condemns a man to death, but a murderer legally ordered to affront God, sport with the everlasting wrath of Divine justice, and trample, with a mortal impunity, upon the most sacred laws of Providence.

72. I am also fully aware of this circumstance, that, by speaking thus, I will shock many persons, and, most likely, run the risk of being upbraided

by them; but, as I think less of shunning censure, than of imparting conviction, if I can; I let my mind render, fearlessly, an exact account of its impressions. Should a whole society oppose me, I would still say that the gospel of Christ stands by my side; the more I read it, the more I find that our criminal codes are a flagrant contradiction, nay, violation of it. No one can, in my opinion, be a sincere Christian who, after having examined duly all the consequences of legal death, can sanction the power granted by the law to erect scaffolds and gallows.

73. In vain will some one say that capital punishment is one of the many necessities which must have been foreseen by God, and, consequently, that divine grace stands always ready to operate as well by legal as by eventual death. Sophisms will not do here. We cannot take it as granted, that God combines the inspiration of his grace so as to make it suit capital punishment which he has not sanctioned; as he may for example, let his heavenly favours fall upon those persons who perish in consequence of an event which he ought to foresee when he decided in his eternal wisdom what should be the laws of the moral and physical orders. He owes it to himself to have his means, either of preservation in this world, or of salvation in the other, always at hand, that none of his acts should, in any way, time, or case, be reprehensible; but he is, in no instance or manner, bound to obey our whims, or govern so as to agree with our passions.

74. On the one side, his grace operates to suit itself; and on the other, human freedom acts as it likes: so, whilst he answers for his deeds, we have to answer for ours. As long as the liberty, which he endowed us with in order that we might journey through the very narrow and often incumbered path of truth, acts in accordance to his holy commands, and endeavours to comply with his will, we tend surely to our natural destination and will, in the end, meet happily with our benevolent and faithful Ruler

according to his promise; but, if we depart from our duty, we depart also from God, and heap, undoubtly, on our heads measures of wrath. No doctrine is purer, and in the same time, clearer than this!

75. Now, does human freedom, when it inflicts capital punishment, abjure obedience to the will of God, and, therefore, provoke his anger? Methinks it does, if we adhere to the principle just expounded in the preceding paragraphs. But, let us suppose that, with respect to this point of public morals, as well as with respect to some others of a mighty importance, a doubt may arise whether man can or cannot inflict death. Shall society, thus left between two hypothesis, of which the result decides the question of eternity for an individual, legalize the right, or rather make it an uncontrovertible right to cut boldly the thread of life when it judges proper to do so? I say it must not. Whilst two honest and equally rational principles conflict, and especially at the foot of the scaffold on which a man is either to be hanged or be beheaded, it is time, or it never will be, to put into practice this wise axiom of Zoroaster: *In the doubt, abstain thyself.* I pass to another argument.

76. Suicide, which every good Christian condemns, is, I believe, less culpable than judicial murder. Though man, by killing himself, infringes the law of God, who commands him to wait patiently here below, until he is called into another world; he commits, after all, no other crime but that which follows from an abuse of the liberty which he enjoys. As it depends upon him to be either good or bad; it depends also upon him to follow either the path to heaven or to hell, as he chooses. But it is not so with judicial murder. It takes upon itself to violate the law of nature with regard to another being, and assumes, let me repeat it again and again, the power of God; therefore, there is no other difference than a conventional one between a judicial and a highway murderer, as both in the abuse of their

liberty involve the life of another, that which the self-murderer does not.

77. Were not suicide a guilty deed, I would easily understand that capital punishment might be inflicted, inasmuch as the law ordering it would result from a social contract, in virtue of which each and every citizen would have transferred to society, for the advantage of all, his individual rights. But suicide is prohibited, both by nature and by the religion of Christ; therefore, society cannot kill, as its members cannot, either collectively or separately, give up their life to the arbitrary decision of another, any more than they can attempt to quit the world by an act of their own.

78. The only plausible argument which one might bring here, is that which is drawn from the right which we have to expose our life in a case of self-defence, and of course, to kill any person who attacks us with intent to kill. It seems that in the same manner as society has the right to arm its members, lead them against its foes, and expose them to death, by enjoining them to oppose those who threaten its existence; so it can arm with the axe of criminal justice a few citizens whose duty it shall be to pursue murderers, and kill them for the sake of securing its tranquility.

79. This argument, no doubt, is specious: but however strong and conclusive it may appear, we must acknowledge that it is not so in reality; for what comparison can we establish between a murderer and a political foe? None whatever. The one is an aggressor whom society is obliged to resist, and the other a malefactor whom it has to punish. The one threatens its constitution, the other is in its hands. Then, by killing the political foe, society defends itself; but by hanging the murderer, it commits an act of revenge; that which is formally prohibited by the Christian law.

80. But let us admit that, in some instances, murderers are as dangerous to society, as a warlike am-

bitious enemy may be; and that, as a celebrated pirate said to Alexander, robbers differ not from conquerors but on account of a difference of power and means. What of that? Shall we conclude that the pirate can be killed when he is a prisoner, because the conqueror can be resisted? Methinks we should not; but, on the contrary, deal with both in the same way, since we place them on an equal footing. Let our constables, men of arms, and other police officers, pursue the thieves and murderers, entrap or fight them if they refuse to surrender, as our soldiers would go and meet in an open field the enemy of our country. Inasmuch as a contest has become necessary to apprehend an evil doer, the case of self-defence is clearly demonstrated, and death may follow from that defence; but in the same manner as we, Christian people receive not from victory the right of killing the prisoners whom we make in war, so we must not order the death of a murderer because we have him in our power.

81. Nature which, in the first case, approves, nay, inspires the feeling of resistance, reproves and stigmatizes, in the other, the desire of vengeance. As long as a villain fights, as it were, hand to hand with the officers of society, he jeopards his life in the same manner as he did in presence of any fellow being whom he dared to attack with an intent to kill; and society, no doubt, can kill him through its officers.—But, when he has been taken into custody, no authority on earth, except that of a barbarous power, can put him to death, without becoming its equal, that is to say, a wilful murderer; because it is no more justice but skill and might which constitute the right which that authority takes upon itself to exercise.

82. Moreover, if society has received from nature the power of executing murderers, murderers can resist it; and if they do resist with advantage, what will become of society?—Now, that murderers will resist society, is a case by no means improbable.

Let us suppose that a riot takes place; murders are perpetrated; society shows itself indignant: but what can it do? Nothing in some instances; for who has made society? Either oligarchy or democracy. If it is oligarchy, rioters will say that they have as much right to destroy as a few citizens may have to establish; and, then, victory alone will decide the result in favour of either side, but not the question of right in favour of the government, the goodness of which cannot depend upon a conquest of this sort. If it is democracy, rioters will maintain that an order of things can, at any time, be undone by those persons who have made it; for that portion of a society which spills blood in riots, thinks that it acts justly, and does actually free the law from difficulty, whilst it prevents the ordinary justice from committing an illegality. So, in either case, the welfare of all is compromised: crime presumes to defend itself: it stands either isolated or opposed to society, whose salvation depends exclusively, either upon a chance of success on the field of battle, or upon a superiority of strength. If it be defeated in the struggle, crime prevails legitimately, that which should not be; and if it triumphs, murder is legalized, which is an abuse of might over incapacity. But the principle remains the same, viz: that criminal punishment is an act of tyranny and not of justice.

83. I would certainly not defend the insurrection of rogues against society. To me as much as to any body else, riots and murders are, indeed, hateful. But I cannot help considering human contingencies such as they are. When society usurps the power of God, the people can usurp the power of society. One single man can endeavour to take from society what society takes from heaven; and, thus, depravity is authorized by a reprehensible example. The principle is caused to vary from the one side to the other, but the scandal ceases not; for the rogue will never acknowledge that he is wrong, as long as

society confesses not that it is unjust. Whilst it prepares and sharpens the deadly weapons with which it kills criminals; criminals, yet free from prison and chains, laugh at society, trample upon its ptetensions, plunder and kill where and whenever they can. A mere game of chance is played by them; they throw the law of society, as society does the law of God, upon a die; win who may! Is that to govern in accordance with the precepts of nature, and, more especially, with those of Christ?

84. I say it is not. Prejudices, sophisms, habits or passions may induce men to believe that they are right when they are wrong; cause them to draw illicit consequences from an evident principle, and lead them from error into crime: but, whenever they will be disposed to act wisely, they can easily distinguish between what is permitted and what is not. For instance, nature tells them that absolute necessity alone allows them to kill their like, and, therefore, that they infringe one of its most important laws, if they murder for motives of contingency, and in virtue of a metaphysical reasoning upon what may or may not suit society. In a case of necessity, things speak by themselves, and God manifests, if so it can be said, his will; whilst in any other, he suggests to man no other rule of conduct except that which orders man never to pass beyond the narrow circle of his capacity. So, whosoever presumes to kill, save when an evident and almost preternatural necessity allows him to do it, sits bodily on the very throne of God, waves his heavenly sceptre over the world, and becomes so much more culpable as he presumes to rise higher, and usurp the eternal power with impunity. I have often thought that all our social miseries grow out of this insolent pretension on the part of man!

85. But, do not villains and murderers commit every day that which, I say, society has prohibited? Yes, they do. Then society can deal with them as they deal with others! No, it cannot; for rascality is no

example to follow; and woe unto a people among whom it would be received as a social guide! Because an outlaw dares to brave heaven and earth, and without caring about the dreadful consequences of his misdemeanor, stabs with a poniard his like to the heart, takes in a felonious manner his life, and hurls, as it were, his soul into the inextricable abyss of eternity, should we authorize society to imitate him? No. We can no more order murder for murder, and blood for blood, than we can permit theft for theft, and rape for rape. Society is established to practice virtue, and not to perpetrate crime under whatsoever pretence. . . . .

86. And, should some persons reply here, that, by stating that society must not retaliate, Philosophy makes the condition of villains actually better than that of society; I will answer candidly that it must be so in some points; for society is, in this sublunary world, just in the same predicament in which God himself is placed in the centre of a free universe. As long as the period of liberty lasts, the condition of the Creator is worse than that of his creatures; the ill-behaviour of whom he has to bear patiently until the time of their death, when he will, in his turn, as the Bible says, mock and insult such of them as have been wicked in this world: *Ego quoque in interitu vestro, ridebo and subsannabo vos.* So should it be with society!

87. The only argument that can be brought, with some appearance of reason to impair this principle, and prove that society may be impatient, though God is not, comes from the essential difference which exists between God and society. The one is for ever, and the other for awhile only; therefore the one can wait, and the other cannot; otherwise things would cease to be on an equal footing. The argument, I say, seems to be conclusive, and is so, indeed; but it is in favour of and not against the principle which I am endeavouring to defend. God is patient, not because he is sure of being able to

punish when he pleases, but because he knows well, and masters with certainty the ultimate results of all things. Should the slightest doubt enter his mind with respect to his own work, he would destroy it instantly, and begin it anew. But he is sure of what he does: any thing which goes out from his hands must be as it is, and is well. Though, for the sake of that meritorious liberty which he imparted to man, he seems to depend upon the accident of an unfinished order, he does, nevertheless, hold firmly in his hands the wonderful series of those innumerable links which unite together all the events of which the motives and effects escape our imperfect sight and limited understanding.

88. Now, is society naturally endowed with such an immense and comprehensive wisdom? No, it is not. What it has once let go, it can no more recall or even find out. Eternity is a realm into which its eyes penetrate not. It is unable to dispose of things out of the narrow compass which an insuperable power has traced around it. There is always a doubt in its mind whether it has acted properly; and it has, often, no remedy whatever for what it has managed wrongly in the beginning. Like man whose real image, or rather personification, it is on a larger scale, it has no influencee whatsoever beyond the grave. So, the very same motives which permit God to punish for ever, because he can, whenever he pleases, revoke his sentence, prohibits society to do it, as it can neither create any thing nor control death. Hence that sacred duty not to be hasty in what it orders, and avoid doing what it cannot mend, which binds it at all times!

89. By cutting the throat of a man, or choking him to death with a rope, society does undoubtedly annihilate him in as much as it can, and, thereby, include eternity itself in that horrid operation: whilst, by punishing murderers so as to make them, first of all, feel a pungent remorse, and, then, undergo such humiliations, suffer such corrections as lay at its dis-

posal, it acts in accordance with the natural order of things which commands it to do the very reverse of what depravity does, and keeps in its right place. When a judge, commissioned to punish a criminal, has abandoned him legally to his own conscience in a dungeon, and heaped around him the toils, hardships, and such bodily chastisements as can be inflicted by man, he has complied with his painful duty honestly, and may take his rest without scruple. God will do what he cannot; I mean inspire the criminal with regrets, or condemn him to everlasting punishment.

90. But I will go still further, and admit that society is actually invested with the power of death and life in a case of murder, as God is. Can it, consequently kill a man legally? I say it cannot; for God, whose authority it assumes, does not kill sinners however depraved and wicked they may be. That passing off, which we call death, is nothing else but the very natural act which causes man to enter from one state of things into another. A mere point placed, as Paschal says, between two mysterious extremes, that is to say, time and eternity; Man drops from the one into the other, but perishes not for ever. Reason, adds the same philosopher, agrees every where with the Christian faith, upon this doctrine. But if such is death; is it not evident that capital punishment is excluded from the code of God? He lets man come out from his hands, endows him with the most absolute liberty, for good or evil; and, then, judges him according to the good use or abuse which he has made of that liberty, chastises, or rewards him eternally, in consequence of the judgment which he obliges him to undergo, but destroys him not on account of his crime.

91. Indeed, it is a topic altogether independent of the one which we examine now, to investigate how and why such is the code of God. But, though we may have to vindicate, in other instances, the Christian doctrine about heaven and hell, we must admit

it here as granted, and reason accordingly. Man, do we say, dies not when his bodily frame ceases to breathe and is reduced to dust, but continues to live for ever in his soul, which for ever remains as it was, either good or criminal, at the time of that solemn and awful separation. He shall be for ever either damned or saved, according to the vices or virtues which he will take with him before the tribunal of his Maker. As long as this doctrine stands, and it will always stand, God will not kill but keep his criminals always alive amidst the sufferings and griefs which he has prepared for them. Why, then, should society, the god of earth, do within its perishable dominions what the true, eternal God, whom it takes as its model, does not choose to do in his everlasting kingdom?

92. I wish earnestly that it was plainly understood that this present life is to society which must finish, what eternity is to God who will never end; and that the former would act here, as the latter does there. In this case, our criminal justice would be altered instantly. Society better enlightened, and actuated by a nobler motive, would be satisfied by isolating in its dungeons, the hell of this world, those men whom it should judge unworthy of enjoying its paradise, which is civil liberty. Then, villains and murderers would be chastised as they should be. Confined within the limits of a terrestrial hell, if I am permitted to say so, they would discover in it what condemned sinners find out, at last, in the everlasting one; that is, a severe justice, a conscience whose remorse cannot die, painful griefs and ever pungent torments.

93. So far as their offences had a reference only to the rights of society which they infringed, their punishment would be fully adequate; and their ultimate destination after life left to their own arbitration. Earth would be satisfied with their earthly sufferings; and heaven would be at liberty to fulfil, at leisure, with them its eternal designs of justice or

mercy, according to their repentance or obduracy. Human justice, by keeping all sorts of tribulations alive, both in their hearts and minds, subjecting their bodies to fatigues, which neither power nor favour should be allowed to alleviate, would weigh, I think, heavily enough upon them; and God should not have to complain, while his power would be respected religiously by society.

94. The only difficulty which may occur even in the respectful and religious application of this principle, is, that man should presume to obtain through it what God alone has a right both to do and expect, since what we owe to man is but a part of what we owe, first, to God. Some philanthropists have, I hear say, succeeded so far as to prevail upon such societies as they were members of, and obtained from their legislation that capital crimes, as we call them, should henceforth be punished otherwise than with death. There should their philanthropy have stopped; for, if they flatter themselves with the hope of contriving a plan which in its identical execution will, at the same time, punish and better convicts, they mistake much.

95. When man, any where or in any way, undertakes to act like God, and interferes, directly, with the divine grace, he runs the risk either to conceive justice wrongly, or, perhaps, to become the support of cruelty. Our intellect is too weak, too narrow, that we may depend upon it as if it was a certain medium through the use of which morality is, consequently, obtained. Presumption, impatience, absolutism itself, are so congenial to our nature, that we are, commonly, hasty in our designs, restless in our pursuits, tyrannical in our efforts, and thus exposed to become, though unwillingly, heartless torturers for the purpose of satisfying our vain expectations.

96. Civil morality has for its object to secure the life, the property and the fame of every individual who is a part of a society. If that society obtains

so much through its legislation, it is enough; as it will suffice, also, if it take care to have either that morality enforced by the law, or its infractors duly punished: but if it presumes to change the thoughts and feelings of the bad citizen whom it punishes, it passes its power; it undertakes more than it can do. Our nature immured according to a sentence, and doomed to a lonesome silence amidst such hard labours as are imposed upon it, however guilty we suppose it to be, shrinks, and submits less through repentance than through fear or necessity. Its obedience, like that of insanity, is caused by the inward feeling of its degradation. The more we pretend to force upon it our views and notions of good and right, the more it proves either reluctant to bend, or hypocritical in its compliance with our wishes or orders. I might call here the whole world as a witness to this proposition: Nothing good can rationally be expected from a man, still less from a villain, who enjoys not his liberty! . . . .

97. Let us look at those countries where slavery is allowed! A master takes into his head to bring down to a mute and passive obedience a slave whose mind refuses to stoop, and whose passions decline to obey. What is to be done? You will see. The master substitutes, for the means of persuasion used until then, iron collars and chains, lashes, hard labour, very severe, nay, cruel castigation, to conquer the obstinacy of the slave. What is the result? That the master finishes by getting, in the mangled person of his slave, either a hypocrite, a madman, a murderer, or, perhaps, a corpse. . . . . . See, also, that eccentric father, who, in his dangerous fits of piety, thinks that there is nothing like a religious severity to make a good Christian of his son! He adopts, accordingly, such means of correction and sanctification as are suggested to him by an ill-understood religion. What fruit is he to reap from an education thus conducted? None, but the contempt of rational men, the hatred of his child, and the wrath

of Heaven, for which he has brought up, most likely, a blasphemer.

98. It is a fact now authenticated, that in the upper classes of society, the unbelievers of both sexes are the very persons whose Christian education was the more severely attended to, and upon whom every sort of religious practices were more strictly enforced; whilst, in the lower classes, lost girls, libertines, rogues of every description, were often brought into the extreme of infamy from the extreme of virtue. In both orders, religion, either forcibly or improperly inculcated in juvenile and passionate hearts, yielded its place, either gradually or at the first essay, to depravity or incredulity.

99. Now, if from the world we go into the sanctuary of priesthood and convents, we will find that the same causes produce the same effects. Inasmuch as the life of a priest, a monk, or a nun, who have become what they are of their own accord, is truly pious and edifying; so, that of the unfortunate creatures, whom a barbarous custom or paternal tyranny have forced into either of those respectable conditions, is scandalous, and tends to confirm the bad opinion which uninformed people entertain about monks and nuns. A man or a woman shu up in a monastery, in consequence of a command contrary to their own will, happen to be in the same predicament with a citizen confined in a state prison, on account of his practical opposition to the government which does, in fact, master his country. Convents can no more make a good monk or a pious nun, than a strong castle can make a democrat of an aristocrat, and, conversely, an aristocrat of a democrat. Religious or Political thought can by no means be mastered.

100. But if constraint has no power upon our minds, still less shall it have over our hearts a salutary influence. That means which is unable to impart belief, cannot, either, infuse virtue. In the same manner as a prisoner of state, when once libe-

rated, will obey his political impressions; or a monk, when set at liberty, give himself up to worldly pleasures, of which we suppose he has been deprived through force; so will the galley slave, whom criminal justice releases, after having detained, punished and isolated him for years in a dungeon, go back to his former habits: that is to say, to honesty, if he was condemned unjustly, or better disposed than he was supposed to be by his judges; or to depravity, if depravity was really the mistress of his heart at the time in which his person was immured in the name of society.

101. We cannot repeat it too often: God alone knows how to enlighten the mind and convert the heart. And when he intends to do so, he never uses other means but that of human freedom, because men are fit only to spoil the work of his divine grace through their peevishness, or even destroy it altogether through their unbearable pride. What can virtue expect from a being who raises confidently his head above the ethereal regions where dwells the Spirit of God, though his common height measures no more than five feet eight inches; whose mind resides within an infinitely small compass, and yet dares to handle presumptuously the eternal thought; whose life, though it is a mere shadow, attempts to shine over society like another sun; whose science should be to ascertain that he knows nothing, but presumes, however, to emulate that of God himself? We laugh at his vain efforts as long as we contemplate them by the light of reason, and pity the fate of virtue thus left to the thousand errors and follies of human weakness and pride; but, as soon as those errors and follies prevail, we submit to them blindly, and follow, like as many sheep, the path beaten by the daily steps of a thoughtless majority. Indeed impertinence may reign kingly where stupidity has become the order of the day!—But it will not last for ever.

102. Between a blameable contempt and a blind confidence in a religious belief as a means of correc-

tion, there is a medium pointed out to us by common sense. We should follow it. As punishments inflicted by the law tend both to chastise the offenders and diminish crimes by the aid of fear; prisons should neither be a den of banditti thrown there, helter skelter, to frighten visiters, nor a dreary solitude where silence and the Bible alone are allowed to enter; but a place in which hard labour should be seconded by a minute and active philanthropy. Free agency must neither be favoured too much nor chained too closely in a guilty conscience; because, in the first case, it would lead to an undaunted depravity; and, in the second, to an useless despair or studied roguery.

103. Some prison reformers have gone so far as to think that, with a stupid turnkey, they can keep in order one hundred convicts. I wish I might abide by their opinion. But reason and experience forbid it. On the one part, I believe not that one single and uniform system can reform a given number of men as easily as well contrived machinery can weave a given number of yards of wool or silk; and, on the other part, I am satisfied that it is impossible to make a trapist of a thief. Egotism, directed by speculation, but not *True Charity*, has hoped to make of a prison a monastery and a monk of a robber, as it is political hatred and not social justice which has dared to make a dangerous criminal of a free thinking citizen.

104. Others flatter themselves that, through a preacher who lets his thoughts flow, at the same time, through one hundred square wickets, remorse and virtue will, like a heavenly whisper or holy dew, either soften the heart or enlighten the mind of a guilty man. They may believe it. I do not; for common sense tells me that the wounds and sores of the human race, whilst depravity attacks it on every side, can no more be cured with the same religious remedy, than all the infirmities to which our bodies are liable, with the same physic or surgical instrument.

105. Such is my conviction!—it results not only from the arguments which have just been expounded, but also from a number of facts which I might quote to confirm them. One will suffice to give a correct idea of all the others, of which it is an example more or less applicable.

There was in the penitentiary of N., which I used to visit, a prisoner whose appearance pleased me. I showed him good will, and soon he repaid it by a feeling of gratitude. He spoke to me about his past life, and I learnt that he had been successively a sailor on board a privateer, a pirate, a coiner of false money, a smuggler, and, at last, a robber.

Depravity was so familiar to him that he could hardly understand why men made a crime of it; and the best reasonings in respect to this topic would not have convinced him. Whether it was an error of his mind, or the effect of corruption in his heart, he laughed at virtue, and maintained that it was but a word or a vain idea suggested to man by the negative condition in which he happens to be, with regard to such feelings and dispositions as may qualify what he calls virtue, by opposition.

I quoted for him many examples of an unsullied probity, of a disinterested religion, of a pure charity, of an admirable chastity, but they were useless. He would shake his head and answer invariably: All that is mere nonsense! Undoubtedly, there existed in the mind of that man a very peculiar philosophy, so much the more important to study, as it appeared to be based upon a real monstrosity—I mean the negation of good, and a firm belief in evil. Therefore I made it a duty to penetrate him thoroughly, no matter what painful efforts it should cost me.

Happily, I had to deal with one of those beings who care not about the judgments of men, and who speak to them without disguise? One day, as I had exhausted the whole chapter of my remonstrances; and he, according to his custom, had laughed at them all; I saw him assume a more serious air at the end of my speech. He left his work, took a seat by me, lowered his head, seemed to be absorbed in some deep reflection, and then, fixing upon me his sullen and bold look, he broke thus his mysterious silence:

"Sir, you must not believe that I was ignorant of such duties as you have been pleased to recall to my mind, supposing that there was ever any thing like a duty. My mother, a woman as severe as she was bigoted—for bigotry never exists but with severity, as far as I know,—took as much care of my childhood, and perhaps more than your own mother did of yours. I can repeat and comment upon the commandments of God and of the church, with such a precision as to astonish the most skilful catechist, and, perhaps, be so eloquent as to be envied by any Christian orator who might listen to me:—but to what purpose such a display of knowledge in a dungeon of twelve feet square! And, besides, what should I tell you that you have not told me already?—it is enough if you are convinced that I am as well informed as you are upon morals, so far as they are explained by men. But there is a science which, it seems, you are unaware of, and which it may be useful for you to learn: It is that of wickedness, or rather of those men whom society calls wicked, for this only reason that they do not agree with it in some points. Listen to me, and when you leave this dungeon, you will have got, most likely, certain information which you had not when you entered here a moment ago!

"When fourteen years old, I found myself on board a privateer; my occupations there, were such as are commonly imposed upon cabin-boys. The slightest fault I committed was immediately punished with the most cruel flogging. My captain and his officers allowed themselves in my presence, many unbecoming liberties which they would not have suffered on the part of the sailors, and for which they used to chastise them severely. I concluded from their extraordinary conduct, that they flogged me not to render me better than I was, but merely to force me to obey blindly, like a beast of burthen; and that the strict submission exacted from the sailors, was for no other purpose than that of securing certain speculations, the objects of which were illegal. On the other hand, I saw the sailors hide themselves whenever they wanted to violate the laws of the vessel; and I was satisfied that they had neither shame nor fear, as soon as they escaped the sight of their superior officers. Consequently, I had no need of a further lesson to believe that evil was but a relative thing. Instructed as I had been, both by a thousand conversatioas and daily examples, I began to imitate the sailors and to deceive my masters; and, I must add, that my first essays succeeded beyond my expectations. I became, soon, as impertinent as my masters, and still more cunning than any of the sailors; so that I was hardly twenty years of age, when I passed for the most perfect rogue on board. Every one admired my progress; but it was not enough for me. I desired to be praised and considered as a prodigy. Now, whereas courage, undaunted courage, was the only means which I had there, to attain this title, I behaved, in many serious encounters which we had with some English vessels, so as to merit the name of a hero, which I received from my equals.

"The captain himself was obliged to acknowledge my superiority, and rewarded it by ranking me among his bravest men; among whom I became, soon, the most celebrated and by far the most formidable. So, whilst nothing important could be done on board without me, I was initiated into all that was passing in it: but this initiation confirmed me in my determination to despise men as I had been despised by them; for it was not virtue which they esteemed in me, but cunning, strength and courage. Had it not been for these three main principles of every wickedness, I should have been for them but a contemptible fool. Fully aware of this circumstance, I made my mind up accordingly, and served them as they wished to be served. I must, however, avow, that this resolution cost me some scruples at first. As I was not yet on a perfect level with the world, and needed to see it nearer, that I might become altogether worthy of it, I would hesitate in some cases; but heaven or hell, as you will choose, came to my aid. Thanks to the good sense, and still better eyes with which nature endowed me, I perceived that my captain was what they call, anywhere else but here in prison, a perfect villain; and I understood that this quality, which many others call a defect, had been the very source of his riches and good reputation among men. He would lie, steal, plunder, kill with the greatest coolness, and all that was well in the eye of the law; because, before he went to his infernal work, he had said publicly: *I will do all that in the name of the king, and for the interest of my country:* just as those celebrated fanatics of former times used to calumniate, to persecute, to imprison, to murder their fellow beings, and congratulate themselves on their horrid deeds in saying: *We do it in the name of the Father, and of the Son, and of the Holy Ghost, and for the sake of the Church, our Holy Mother.*

"Such an example proved, beyond a doubt, to me, that crime was crime but relatively, and convinced me of what I had supposed, viz: that success alone justifies man, and that prejudice is the habitual ruler of our judgments. Consequently, I entered boldly the career which my captain followed with the special consent of society; but, instead of becoming a privateer, and obliging myself to share with society the produce of my plunder, I resolved to turn a pirate, that I might enjoy alone all the treasures which I hoped I would amass. A full success attended my exertions, and I, whom you see now so poor, have robbed and possessed millions. As they cost me many troubles and dangers, I dared to use them as if they had been acquired honestly. Unfortunately, treasures thus gained last not long. I lost them all in gambling and dissipation. What was I to do then? To become a pirate again. My intentions were to start for St. Malo, when I met, in the Elysian fields at Paris, one of my former companions. I made him acquainted with my position. He proposed to me to join a band of counterfeiters, of whom he was one. I accepted, as I thought that robbery was no more a crime on land than at sea. Then, behold me coining false dollars, false Napoleons! The trade went on wonderfully; I had all that I wanted, and I would have continued so until death, if our band had not been discovered, tracked, and dispersed by justice: nay, it happened that one of us was taken, judged, convicted, beheaded! As I was afraid to share his fate, I fled, and took refuge in a remote corner of the Pyrenees. A gang of smugglers whom I met with there, offered me a comfortable asylum, if I would help them. I asked for no better bargain; and God knows what a fortune I might have made in their company, if the peace of one thousand eight hundred and fifteen had not put an end to our plundering. They set on our heels soldiers who, accustomed to face the cannon on a field of battle, feared not to encounter a few smugglers. So, we had to yield; and each one of us retired with the money he had made. I know not where the others went. As for me, I took my way back to Paris, the only place of resort for industry like mine. I had but little, but it would have sufficed, had I been willing to use it moderately. But, moderation is no part of my inclination; I lived like a lord, whilst I was on the look-out to find a company of men who would have no objection to enrich themselves at the expense of their neighbours. Several months elapsed, and I had not been able to discover what I sought. My funds diminished sensibly in the mean time; and, not knowing what to do in Paris, I thought of going to some province where chance might make me encounter what I had not found in the capital. This unhappy resolution brought me here. I will tell you how.

"Among the gentlemen who travelled with me in the stage, there was one whose purse was filled with doubloons; I thought I might as well take possession of them if I could. Consequently, feigning to have some business in the place at which he stopped, I stopped also, and put up at the same hotel with him. The next morning, when he awoke, he found that he had been robbed of his gold. I was suspected and arrested; my pockets were searched, and the gold found in them; I was judged, sentenced, and sent here for five years. Three of these years have elapsed: two more, and I am free. Then I will see what I can do to better my condition; but, depend on it, my dear sir, I will no more expose myself for such a trifle as I have mentioned. Whilst a privateer, I have committed, with impunity, a thousand horrors; As a pirate, I was always successful in my criminal undertakings; The very dangerous trade of a counterfeiter enriched me. I have gained, during my career as a smuggler, a sufficient capital to live upon comfortably; and for the theft of a few doubloons, I have become a galley-slave. Indeed, that is degrading! They shall not catch me at it any more, for I am determined to brave the gallows. I will be a rich lord, or be hanged. No other resource is left for me now, as you may believe!"

So did he speak! it was in vain that I represented to him what object the law intended in punishing him; it was in vain that I exhorted him to comprehend society better, and resolve to become an honest man; he would keep account neither of my good counsels, nor of our judicial morals. I left him, and retired with a deep sorrow in my heart, and sombre thoughts in my mind. Had any person questioned me then, I would have said: "certainly that man is doomed to end, sooner or later, on a scaffold, his flagitious life." But I would have been wrong, for the grace of God operated in him one of those mysterious changes which set at defiance all human wisdom.

As I passed *Roule* street in Paris, some four or five years afterwards, I again met with that extraordinary being. He stood on the threshold of a gunner's shop. I approached, he recognised me, and, taking my hands affectionately, begged me to walk in. At first, I must confess, I hesitated through fear of falling into some snare; but this fear did not last. After having introduced me to a young woman, who, he said, was his wife, and of whom the appearance was altogether modest and agreeable, he offered me a chair, and resumed thus, if I am allowed to say so, the history of his life:

"You may remember, my dear sir, that I was disposed to re-enter the way of crime, as soon as I was liberated from prison: well! God would not permit it. A few days after my return to Paris, I fell sick in the house of a woman who was in the habit of lodging vagabonds like me: that woman, to tell the truth, was a very bad character; but she had a daughter who was as wise and good as she was abandoned. I was left to her care by the mother, who could not help rambling about town to meet with rogues of all descriptions. As long as my sickness lasted, I had a thousand occasions of noticing how patient, how tenderly solicitous, how truly charitable my young nurse was; and my imagination, which gets easily inflamed, would see in her but an angel whom it was pleased to worship. The poor child lavished upon me so many attentions, and showed herself so desirous to content me, that I could not help questioning her, to know how she had become so good, so gentle, so careful, in a word, so adorable." "Alas!" replied she, "it is not me whom you should interrogate, but God. Ever since I heard Father McCarthy preach upon the thoughts and feelings of Jesus Christ, I took pleasure in studying the life of this merciful and compassionate Saviour of men. I read it attentively, and I saw that he delights in forgiving our sins, as much as he likes to see us good and pious; his conduct towards the adulterous but repentant woman, and, especially, his affection for the converted robber who died by his cross, touched me. I threw myself at his feet, persuaded that he would look favourably upon me, if I would abandon the path of sin for that of virtue. I implored his grace sincerely, and asked his pardon for the only shameful fault which I had committed; he granted it to me through the sacrament of penance; and since that time, I adore, I pray, I endeavour to imitate him. It is through love for him and to obey his command, that I am good towards you; then you must be grateful to him, but not to me his poor and humble servant."

"The admirable simplicity, and unaffected religion of that new Magdalen moved me deeply, resumed the old convict. I shed tears, whilst she spoke. I sobbed, and believed in virtue almost spontaneously. I was pleased to listen to the religious words which she read out of Thomas A'-Kempis' book. It seemed to me, that those unknown words read by her gave to my ideas a new and better turn, for I felt that I was no more the same.

'Meanwhile, I was recovering, and the first use I made of my restored health, was to go and visit, with her, the priest whose sermons had converted her. That venerable man welcomed me with an extreme goodness. He spoke much of God, and very little of men; so that I found myself in presence of heaven only. The sight and morals of it pleased me. I submitted to its will. I confessed that I was a sinner. I repented. I vowed a better life. I began it. God, I hope, will forgive me; for, ever since I desired to become reconciled with him, I have done my best to turn a good Christian, that is to say, an honest man.

"This happy change was agreeable to her who had contributed to it. She loved me as I loved her, and we were married in church, the blessings of which have rendered our union happier. We work heartily together, and give to the poor the two-thirds of our profits, with the intention of returning, through this means, at least, a considerable portion of my ill-acquired wealth. Indeed! you were in the right, my dear sir! There is no true felicity for man, except in the practice of virtue, as also, there is no real virtue but through the grace of God, a grace which men can, by no means, impart. Undoubtedly, those good sisters of charity, who took care of me in jail, were as kind and attentive as my wife could be. But I was a prisoner, and as such was disgusted with human nature. No power could have converted me then. But when I was free, when the sweet influence of a pure virtue refreshed me on the bed where I was lying, and assisted by a creature whose cares were evidently disinterested, I felt that I thought for myself. Contented and happy with this precious freedom, I yielded to such inspirations as came to me through religion and probity. Liberty! my dear sir, liberty! through it only, man can be either good or bad."

This anecdote needs no comment. Any one may see that it confirms fully all the reflections which I have made above.

106. It remains only to say that they are for the exclusive use of those persons who believe in our Christian religion, and are pleased to practice it. If among them, some are to be found who differ from me, I have nothing more to tell them, except that there is no opinion, not even a doctrine which cannot be attacked by a sophism. The same mind which comprehends fully the proofs upon which rests the demonstration of the existence of God, comprehends also those which overthrow that demonstration, and make of the most important truth for all, the matter of a doubt for many. No wonder, therefore, if that monstrous mother of falsehood and truth, metaphysics were to bring forth, in favour of capital punish-

ment and biblical corrections, such reasonings as will give abundant satisfaction to lazy jailers, and grant a happy rest, nay, judicial honour to hangmen. As for me, who have published this my opinion not with a certainty that it should be welcomed by all, but with the hope of awakening, at least, a salutary doubt in the minds of believers, and freeing them from inward troubles, by saving them from a murderous act, I conclude this first part with the expression of my sincere wishes for the happy reformation of the religious notions of such as will persevere using the gallows, like kings use arms, as the only decisive argument; and I enter into the philosophical and practical exposition of my subject.

CAPITAL PUNISHMENT.

PART SECOND.

1. Did the human race ever enter into a social contract? Such is the main question to put and solve in order to ascertain whether society has or has not the right of inflicting capital punishment. Now, I dare answer, first of all, that the very idea of a primary contract, in consequence of which men should have aggregated here or there for their common welfare, is, at the same time, groundless and foolish, if not scandalous. Such a state of mind as is necessary to think of a social contract, requires many repeated experiments and positively established facts which men are unable to obtain and analyze, as long as they are isolated and unknown to each other.

2. Convinced of this truth, I have looked for another supposition, which might agree better with reason, and found that among all the histories respecting mankind, the Mosaic account, setting apart its rights to our pious belief, was, evidently, the most probable; and that our race entered naturally into society as soon as it was created both male and female. As to the doctrine which represents our first parents, whosoever they were, as being perfect strangers to each other, scattered at random all over the earth, doomed to live, at first, like beasts in thick forests, and then to associate gradually for the purpose of becoming civilized, by the aid, as it were, of a pic-nick of concessions and knowledge, I consider it quite erroneous. It may be interesting and seducing in poetry, but in good and plain prose, betrays a tough absurdity. Men modify the state of society, but they cannot invent it.

3. The evidence of this fundamental axiom results from the necessary fact, that the use of his tongue is as natural to man and as spontaneous as that of his eyes and ears. The blind and the deaf and dumb are indeed extraordinary freaks of nature, which, as we cannot explain them, enter not into the series of our social calculations. Man, such as he is, with the perfect and happy advantage of his five senses, is the only criterion which we ought to consult. To every philosopher who studies him well, he seems to speak inwardly his thoughts before he thinks of uttering them, and to utter them in the same manner as he sees, smells, acts, and feels, that is to say, naturally, and almost unaware of what he is about, until associations of ideas, comparisons, reflections, all gathering in his mind, afford him some certainty.

4. So, such philosophers as have pretended to honour society with the invention of speech, confounded the gift of thought and speech with the subsequent developement of both in society, and with the various changes to which they are liable in consequence of a free agency. Like that eccentric thinker who, abusing the admirable principle of Descartes, imagined that he had actually got hold of the primary condition of our kind, because he had isolated himself mentally from every thing, and said: Behold me! here I am on the point from which my nature started! I handle now the thread of my existence, and follow it surely through the labyrinth of casuality! They think that they have discovered the natural nullity of the individual, because they found that he was feeble, uncertain and incapable out of society: and in this illegitimately deduced conclusion, their mistake lays!

5. If man had not been able, and had not spoken naturally, his union with his like would not have been more profitable to him than that of other animals with their respective kinds. In vain do these meet together; they neither speak nor improve, because speaking and improving are no part of their

nature. Man, on the contrary, because he possesses, through his, the power of speech, improves himself by communicating with his fellow beings. Like the other works which he can perform with any of his senses, his speech becomes clearer, better and better every day, but enjoys this advantage only in consequence of its pre-existing, like the various objects of our handywork and mental researches, before the use which man may make of it.

6. In proportion as his thoughts increased by the contemplation of external objects, struggled amidst the inspirations imparted to his mind, stretched themselves over the whole creation and its mysteries; his speech, too, extended, grew, improved for the better; he made, at first, words, phrases, sentences of various forms and length; then, those words, phrases and sentences, having varied according to times, places, sensations, events, essays of all sorts, assumed also a special or more determined character. Hence languages and their differences! unless we prefer to explain the mystery of their origin through the wonder of Babel; that which is, by the by, the shortest, and most likely the best way of accounting for it, since we neither do nor shall ever know any thing positive with respect to that grand question. It is as well to solve a mystery through another, as to spend a very precious part of our life in inquiring about a matter of which it will always be correct to say, as Horace says of the inventor of the Elegiac verse, *Grammatici certant; et adhuc sub judice lis est.* From the moment I felt convinced that it is not society that invented speech, but, on the contrary, the faculty of speech that gave birth to society, I must be satisfied that I am something more than a mere animal.

7. But, if man speaks naturally, and, therefore, tends naturally to exercise this noble faculty, it is evident that society, which is a means of communication between man and man, did actually exist previous to any social contract, as we term it. If

man spoke before he knew the extent of his thoughts, and, therefore, the means of combining his own views with the views of others, he lived really in society before he compromised in any way with his like. This practical reasoning is, in my opinion, equivalent to a demonstrated axiom or well authenticated fact.

8. By referring the origin of society to such a beginning, we explain, easily enough, all its wrongs; whilst, by establishing it before-hand upon a contract framed for the purpose, we cannot help stating, at the same time, that men were then actuated by insanity; that which would not be very honourable for our forefathers. But, I must elucidate the proposition: if society is a necessity imposed upon mankind by nature, we understand perfectly well that, in consequence of the defects which it has left in us, weakness will try to lay snares to strength, and strength to trample upon weakness; that intrigue must prevail sooner or later upon simplicity; poverty be made a sort of a stigma; riches give birth to pride, by creating a distinction of classes; the dazzling deeds of a hero thwart the common progress; the laws become, after many revolutions, a repertory of contradictions and means to defraud; justice be used as a medium of oppression, whilst it turns into a source of quirks; war be called a glorious occupation; death pass for the best of all social or political reasons; in a word, disorders of all kinds result from the social order. This is the almost necessary consequence of our natural disposition to either be imposed upon, or to impose upon others; and, to avow it humbly, of that mysterious imperfection which, we know not why, weighs heavily, indiscriminately, continually upon our kind.

9. I do also, thanks to our condition, understand clearly the deplorable defects of the various governments upon which my sight may rest. Since men are the same every where and at all times, republics cannot be much better than monarchies, because

republics, as well as monarchies, are inventions of men. I see it, but am not shocked at it. Every doubt, every perplexity, every indignant feeling I answer calmly with these axioms: No wonder! It must be so! There is no use to censure! Time, reason, or perhaps caprice only can mend all that!

10. But, if society is the result of a primary contract made by men who should understand their rights, please to tell me what I must think, and you too, reader! of a set of free, rational beings, who, whilst they meet together for the common welfare, lay down as a fundamental principle this tyrannical motto: *Might makes right:* acknowledge the inequality of condition, the distinction of classes, the abuse of the paternal authority, the resistance of children to their parents, the necessity of running to an almost certain death to oblige a king, create either an oligarchy or a democracy, conquer a ditch or a mound of earth, win a few pieces of gold or a few acres of land, avenge an insult totally immaterial to the interest of mankind? What are we to think of men coming, by thousands and thousands, to agree upon the means which they have to take, in order that they may cheat each other more surely, load themselves with chains for the theft of a trifle, and crown their heads with laurels for the plunder of a province, call themselves executioners when they hang a man, and heroes when they kill their like by millions on a field of battle? What are we to think of these wise leaders of men, who, after having duly studied, as it is supposed, their passions, and found that their propensity to evil is nearly as powerful as their tendency to good; that vice has, like virtue, its many chances of success; and that crime is to be determined more by the intention than the fact; dare, nevertheless, to enact such laws as will admit of no distinction; strike at random, kill for the best, say yes or no, in the most mighty cases, according to the mental power of a small being called magistrate, or of a few individuals gathered hastily in a street and

commissioned to represent wisdom and justice in every civil and criminal case?

11. Indeed, that is sufficient to show that society derives not its existence from a social contract. The power of man over woman, of a father over his children, of the eldest son in a family, of the ablest among his brothers, of the most courageous or intelligent in his tribe: such has been the origin of society! In consequence of their quarrels, antipathies, hatreds, divisions among themselves, men did, afterwards, form, without any preliminary understanding, societies which became as many strangers to each other. Created by God to be the numberless members of a vast, but single family, they cheated the purpose of their Maker by unmaking themselves, not through a motive of virtue, but in compliance with the dangerous commands of their passions. Hence the scattering of so many nations over all the earth! Hence wars and usurpations of all sorts! Hence the differences of language, laws and manners in different countries!

12. Instead of recording these remarks, and pronouncing that men did constitute themselves into a society, but in pursuance of their determination to oppose the existing order of things—some philosophers have judged it more fashionable to decide in favour of a social contract made and signed at some unknown period of past ages. May God bless them! but their pretended contract is a mere hoax, at which they laugh themselves. The tendency to unite with his like, which is congenial to man, dates from his cradle, and will last to the end of things, in spite of any form of government which may be introduced to facilitate the progress of his kind, towards that said to be better order of things, which we call civilization.

13. I will even dare to add, that civilization, far from improving at all times the condition of mankind, has, in a measure, made it worse, whilst it was abused like all the other means of perfection left to

the discretionary power of man. Those nations who never were visited by it, struggle with common errors only; but such as have been acquainted with it, saw often those errors changed into laws, and falling back upon them with an increased weight. The former stand firm, still waiting for better days. The latter stagger more or less along the brink of a political precipice. Moreover, the periods of liberty endure not so long as those of absolutism, because, whilst liberty leads often to licentiousness, absolutism decreases slowly, and by its gradual decay, supplies men with an ever new occasion of delight.

14. But, we have not to question civilization. It is the beginning of the social thread that we are looking after, to comprehend what reform society stands in need of. Where is that beginning? With the patriarchal state. Let us go back to it; for no where but in an unbiassed thought, or in that of an honest, upright father really resides the sound doctrine of justice, of which the object is to manage properly indulgence and severity, the main hinges on which every social order has to move. Multifarious opinions, resulting from a conflict between interests opposed to each other, never produce but monsters. Men state that they are brothers, and deal like perfect strangers with each other. They say that they are but one family, and refuse to recognise the same father. And so it will be as long as they decline to retrace their steps.

15. Whatever may be the constitution of a people, the position is the same with respect to a proper government. Republics, kingdoms, monarchies, oligarchies, and democracies, these are mere names, forms, or shadows. Let them be what you please, but have a care that the principle which is to govern any of these societies be kept pure and always alive. Enact such laws as an equitable father would sanction. Consider each other as children who expect either a due reward for their merits, or a just castigation for their faults. Let your code be posi-

tive and plain, for societies which cannot support themselves without constables, men-of-arms, and sheriffs, are liable to many abuses.

16. Look at the paternal administration? A father does not kill his son, because this son has killed a brother. He does not enrich himself with the property of two of his children in order to decide in favour of which of the two justice stands. He does not bury alive in a dungeon that one of the family who has committed a theft, nor does he dishonour him for a foible. Why, then, do you these things ye men who live in society?—because you have become strangers to one another. When the guilty citizen whom your criminal law has attainted, is one of your own family, you say that those laws are too severe, you accuse them of being cruel and arbitrary. Perhaps you are in the right! But when the culprit is unknown to you, what do you look at, if not the law alone and the crime which it punishes, since you say then: Pursue that wretch, judge him, convict him, hang him without mercy! Is such a conduct the proof you would give of a social contract?—undoubtedly not. Change, then, your laws, and choose another principle of government!

17. Every man who has to contribute his knowledge for the formation of a criminal code, should, first of all, remember that he works for himself, then for his family, relations, or friends, and, at last, for his like. Does he do it? No: on the contrary, he follows the trodden path, and gives his mind up to a pretended political agreement which habit has authorized: he lets cruelty usurp the rights of justice, because some bloody tyrants or stupid thralls have declared a long time ago, that the law should have neither heart nor soul, but live exclusively in its letter; and, instead of trampling upon this wicked axiom, he loses his time in analyzing legally its consequences, making of them as many laws, and contriving means to have them mercilessly fulfilled. A

worthy occupation indeed! most especially where humanity and wisdom boast of their influence!

18. Shall we found, then, our social order upon the sanguinary example which the first and the last Brutus set to their fellow citizens in Rome? Shall we say that they must be imitated, those two monsters, of whom the one beheaded his children, and the other stabbed his father? Then, also, we will rule our societies after the barbarous will of an infanticide and the passions of a parricide. But who would dare to praise those two Roman villains?

19. The axe of Brutus, the father of a new-born republic, was no more serviceable than the dagger of Brutus, the defender of a decayed democracy, to the triumph of liberty. She arose from amidst the shameful lust of Tarquinius, and expired smothered under the laurels of Cæsar. Thus explained, her birth and death are more honourable with respect to Rome, and better understood by us; for, whilst pride is pleased to discover the causes of a grand revolution in a few crimes decorated with the name of public virtue; wisdom sees that it resulted from events, the combination of which changed it into a necessity.

20. Men, therefore, should cease to pay a respectful attention both to those violations of the natural law, which some of the pretended great men of antiquity committed, and to those sophistical doctrines which were taught by some dogmatic and erring philosophers, who, misled by their admiration for any thing which is extraordinary, praised crime, and departed from humanity in the various codes which they proposed to govern society. Nature alone should be consulted. How would a father act, if he had to decide upon a case which is brought before our courts? Such is the question which we must put, first of all, to ourselves; and, then, answer it honestly for the purpose of coming nearer and nearer to truth!

21. Paternal legislation, if I understand it well, knows neither cruelty nor self-interest; by it, conse-

quently, exile or transportation does away with murderers, thieves, counterfeiters, and libertines; by it also, temporary isolation, some salutary correction, which may cause shame and not dishonour, and reasonably proportioned fines or humiliations, correspond with crimes of a less importance, such as reprehensible though not altogether criminal deeds and wrongs, which tend either to deprive one's neighbour of his property, or hurt his reputation. On another hand, paternal legislation consults with the same care about the interests of both the offender and the offended, as it does about the material advantage of society at large. It spends public monies not to build up splendid prisons or blood-smelling scaffolds, but to provide for the transportation of convicts; it holds incorrigible culprits as madmen, whom it shuts up carefully, or as blood-thirsty savages, whom it keeps far from its social borders; it believes not in the supposed tendency of villains to increase their number, because experience tells it that human nature, though feeble and liable to many defects, is, nevertheless, friendly enough to virtue; and, therefore, that the number of evil-doers shall always be comparatively small among men; it trusts public morals much more than it does the effect of a sword or a club used against wicked men in other societies; and endeavours, above all, to diminish crimes by putting a check upon luxury, the mother of envy, libertinism and theft, enforcing probity in contracts, saving the poor from the dangerous contempt of the rich, preventing intrigues from working the ruin of honest people, and ambitious associations from breaking down private industry.

22. Every one, I think, will acknowledge that this is a laudable occupation, and that a legislation carried on on such a principle, must be good; but, if it is good, ours, so far as it is the absolute negation of it in practice, must be bad; and so it is! We have started from this principle, that men out of whom society is made, have reached the age of *majority*, and are,

thereby, freed from every family bondage, so that it becomes their right to be governed in society, otherwise than they should be in their family. The principle is clear, but its consequences are perilous, inasmuch as they may lead to a full abjuration of every feeling of humanity properly so called.

23. By viewing each other as strangers, the citizens of a country insensibly arm themselves against each other through either ambition, pride, envy, intrigue, or mere antipathy. They avail themselves of a vain equality before the law, to confirm, practically, their ruinous tendency to a distinction of ranks in society, and never are so distant from one another in their social intercourse, as when they pretend to enjoy a perfect equality in politics. It seems that a reciprocal contempt springs from their respective conditions, and that they meet only to give to such as are rich or dignitaries of state an occasion of haughty exultation, and to those who are poor or tradesmen a perpetual motive of discontent and hatred.

24. Thus, when they have to redress wrongs or correct culprits, it is not a hope of amendment, but the despicable egotism of revenge which actuates the enactment of their criminal law. They say not, how shall we do, what course shall we take to better that unfortunate offender? but, how shall we get rid of him, how shall we torture him? They say not, let us look for a remedy that may either put an end to murder, or impair its bad effects, with regard to both the murderer and the family of his victim! But, let us kill, hang, behead the villain! The rest is no business of ours!

25. Indeed, by this monstrous way of proceeding, nothing is so easy as to demonstrate that the actual condition of society is so deplorable only because we do not understand liberty, and abuse it most shamefully! Persuaded that it was granted to us by God for the purpose of guiding our actions, we presume that we can use it as we please, provided we revere God; and we think that all is said, judged, decided,

when we have inscribed at the beginning of our constitutions these memorable words: *God and liberty;* and when we have stated that the voice of the people is the voice of God, *vox populi vox dei.* But these two mottoes mean not what they seem to purport according to our misled judgment. Let us comment them?

26. God and liberty!—How can men associate as making one only, two principles which often contradict each other?—What is God where absolute liberty prevails? A mere subject of controversy, which pride and ignorance presume to investigate and divide, each according to his notions. Then, where liberty prevails there is no God, or rather none can claim him as an authority. If we have God in that sense that we make him interfere in our political debates, we have no liberty, as the first use which we must, religiously speaking, make of it, is to submit blindly its action to the will of God; and if we have liberty, God is nothing but an abstract cause, which is, for all, a motive of reflection, but not a certain rule of conduct, unless he does actually manifest himself in some way or other, that every one shall be obliged to recognise. All that is evident. Therefore, let us not affirm that, because we believe God the author of our liberty, we can use that liberty as we choose. A faculty, which, by its nature, may err, should not be identified with truth itself. One God in heaven and liberty on earth, I understand it well. But God and liberty mixed together, so that liberty can develope itself according to its essence, and, however, remain united with the divine match which we give it; that I do not understand, for this plain reason, that it cannot be. Otherwise, there would be no action of society that should be reprehensible on this score, that each of its actions results from liberty. But we know that society may be and is often in the wrong. Therefore it is not, in many cases, with God, though it is always with liberty; and, as it never can ascertain whether God is or is not with

it, in the laws which it enacts, it should not say, God is the justifier of my liberty; or, in the usual words, *God and liberty!*

27. The other axiom, *vox populi vox dei*, is still more defective. Every one will say so, who looks attentively at its ridiculous and terrible consequences. If it were true, God would be, at the same time, the author of the Braminical and Turkish faith. Out of his unchangeable mind would alternately proceed the mythology of Greece and Rome, and the thousand different ways of understanding the creed of Christ. He would have acknowledged as his equals the vegetables of Egypt and the wooden idols of the pagan nations. The death of Christ in Judea, and the Christian wars would be his work. By him, also, nations would arm against each other, spill blood, undertake dangerous revolutions, and truth and falsehood be and be not what they are according to times, notions and places, for all that was and is not but through the will or voice of the people.

28. No. Liberty is, by no means, the companion of God; and God walks not always along with the people. Religion, the end of which is to subdue human will, and errors which, from the origin of societies, sprung numberless from our deviation from divine will, bear testimony that we have sacrificed the necessity of submitting in our social institutions to the invariable law of nature, to the right of resisting tyranny, (which right nobody denies, but which is often ill understood,) and to the liberty of being good or bad which we have individually inherited. Then in order to extricate ourselves from every difficulty or reproach, we have confounded the infraction with the duty, the abuse with the right; and, out of this impious mixture, have come the various monsters of legislation which we see, now and then, among men!

29. But, if civil legislation has thus turned to be, in many places, the poisonous fruit of ambition and tyranny, when they had conquered probity and re-

ciprocity, which insisted, at all times, that we should be satisfied with the primary family legislation, or rather instinctive law of nature; it is equally evident that our criminal codes are a barbarous idea ingrafted in the same law, for they are no more the expression of a justice established to save reciprocity among men, but a mere instrument of cruelty, invented to content violent passions, and handed by the law to vengeance. Hence the name of *vindicta publica*, which we give to capital punishment! So it is true, as our Bible says, that iniquity cannot conceal its real object. *Mentita est iniquitas sibi.*

30. Let us, however, set all these considerations aside, and admit, as they say, through a *dato non concesso*, that such a social contract as is generally understood, was made in the beginning of society! Does it follow from an agreement entered into by men concerning the power of life and death, that they had a right to confer such a power upon society? No, indeed! Reason may die in one man, and, perhaps, linger in a society, the greatest part of which is governed by the passions of a few devoted to tyranny; but it cannot perish altogether, so long as our whole race is not doomed to depart from truth. Now, that reason tells us that we come from a first cause; that man, who cannot endow himself with life, cannot either dispose of it, and that we must live here below patiently until the power which has created us is pleased to take us somewhere else. Consequently with this universal doctrine, the generality of men condemn suicide. How, then, dare they to contradict themselves, and base the right of punishing with death, which they assume in a body, upon a right which, as they confess, no one of them enjoys individually?

31. Whether there was a social contract or not, the principle remains: one cannot give what he has not; man has not the right of killing; he cannot impart it, unless he is especially commissioned for this purpose by God. We have ascertained in the

first part of this disquisition, that God meddles not with either the civil or criminal administration of society. Then, capital punishment is altogether a violation of the divine power, a flagrant abuse of human liberty, and a hateful act of bloody vengeance!

32. But, it is less amidst the metaphysical archives of our legislative assemblies, the dry text of our codes and the legal formulas of our courts of justice, that we must study a criminal legislation, than in the fearless or dejected conscience of a culprit, the dreadful silence of his cell, and the mournful preparations for his execution. It is in such a place and in such a time that capital punishment must become the object of our horror; for there only can we interrogate it, analyze, measure, and weigh it, such as it has been made by human cruelty.

33. "I will tell you," said a Catholic clergyman to me, whose charity and zeal have been for years proverbial in many prisons of his country, "nothing but what a sad and practical experience have taught me on this painful subject.

"I have for many years dealt, as it were, with galley slaves, prisoners, and criminals of every description; the sighs, the groans, the blasphemies of crime are, I may say, familiar to my ears. Often have I weighed, in my trembling hands, the chains which tied to a damp wall in their solitary dungeons, those living victims whom an ignominious death waited for, and trampled upon the damp straw of their couch, on which lay remorse and despair. Often have I, with the cross of salvation in my hands, and the sorrow-soothing name of Jesus on my lips, interrogated all that depravity and wickedness take a culpable delight in working within human hearts and minds. Then, crime would appear face to face before me. I was made able to handle it at leisure through confession, to strain it, drop after drop, in the hollow, deep, vengeance-weighing scale of heavenly justice, when it was not given to me to frighten it and deliver it, with a consoling feeling of hope, to the benevolent care of an infinite mercy. All those heart renting griefs, which a sensible philosopher, Victor Hugo, has so sadly but so energetically described, passed before me, frightful to contemplate, horrid to analyze. From the bench of a pitiless judge who flung, with a cold boldness, those abandoned and doomed villains, whom society curses, into the abyss of shame and despondency, they fell into my hands ready to receive them at the brink of eternity. I was their last resourcé, their last friend, and they would lean on me as they were dragged from the tribunal, where infamy had reached them and stamped their forehead with the seal of death, into the gloomy cell where heavy fetters awaited their exhausted limbs, and an incessant remorse their humbled minds. Oh! God, what a sight! What painful sensations I had to bear, when, sitting in awful silence by them, I was condemned to listen to the benighted shrieks of their powerless iniquity, to the infernal oaths of a desperate culprit, then reduced either to fear death or to brave its thundering threats! They would, by turns, sink mute and oppressed within themselves, or raise to heaven their insulting looks, shake their irons with an incredible madness, or fall senseless at my feet, drench with bitter tears the bread which an inexorable justice had sent to them to keep them alive until the hour of their execution, tear it to pieces with their poisoned teeth, spit it on the walls which, for ever, separated them from the eyes of liberty and crime. I might see, as they came out and went in, their fears, illusions, prayers, doubts, deceptions, contempt, hatred, and horror of mankind. With them, I counted the days, the hours, nay, minutes and seconds, which brought them, nearer and nearer, to the scaffold. They would seek a refuge in my arms, repose on my breast, breathe upon my heart, implore my pity, thank my charity, when jailers, turnkeys, and police officers, stood afar from them; and cling with all their might to my shuddering body when the hand of the executioner, passing around their neck, caused them to shrink. At last, the time-piece which measured the shortened period of their life, having struck the hour, I would cross with them the threshold of that prison lately so horrible and now so dear to them; bid with them a sorrowful farewell to the prisoners of whom they envied the pitiable fate; look at the stupid crowd which showed itself curious to see despair, blood, and death; ascend, before an irritated God and cruel men, those disgusting boards which no honest carpenter will put up, and no honest man dares to touch; see a sanguinary brute, whom we call an executioner, preparing, like a vile and remunerated murderer, the instrument of death. At that formidable moment, a new, though very short era used to begin for them!—they stood either shaking or firm on their legs, pale with fear or red with anger, dejected or bold, repentant or obdurate, between heaven and hell.—Always frightened during this last period of my painful task, I would tremble, pray, raise to God my eyes, wet with tears, and, then, look again at the unfortunate cause of my sufferings. Alas! he was no more; the blow was struck; death had done its work; and left but a corpse to satisfy the despicable curiosity of the bystanders.

34. "Then, as I retired, I saw either a roughly cut coffin, or a blood-stained basket, which were waiting, at the foot of the scaffold, for the strangled or beheaded body of the victim. Those portable tombs soon received its broken or divided limbs, which a rope, wheel, axe, or any other instrument, had mangled and prepared for the worms in an unconsecrated ground, as every one refuses to lie by the grave of a culprit who descended into it from a scaffold. Women, children, old and young men, hurried around that rotten, blood-dropping sink of human justice, showed themselves anxious to know its loathful secrets, and moved, like the billows of a tormented sea over the wrecks of a thun-

der-struck pirate-boat, from every side of the square, in which they had assembled to witness the execution, to gape over that cadaverous relic of public revenge, until, in order to conclude the tragedy, a sepulchral voice raised slowly from a group of constables, and let these insulting words fall over the multitude: Off! off! ye living wretches, off! and let the justice of God pass on its way! . . . Eternal powers! The justice of God in a dark cell of six feet by twelve! The justice of God, on a few boards put up so as to help the purpose of a blood-thirsty retaliation! The justice of God, in the strangling knot of a rope, or the cleaving edge of an axe! The justice of God, in an oblong box, called a coffin, or a vile, hollow wicker-work lined inside with a coarse skin! The justice of God, amidst rusty chains, ever whetted knives, ready made gallows, or scaffolds, which an executioner has to watch over and keep at the disposal of criminal courts! . . . Has madness or depravity thus prevailed in society, and made of mankind a new race of ferocious animals?"

35. Thus spoke the priest! And that he spoke the truth I have no doubt. In condemning a man to a violent and untimely end, society commits three very distinct crimes, each of which should meet with a severe castigation from a greater power. What are they? First of all, the right which it gives to a citizen, by nature bound to commiserate with his kind, of attacking a man publicly, exposing him, and asking with impunity for his death. Secondly, the act of loading with despair and chaining, I may say, in the horrible necessity of a criminal pride, the culprit whom it feeds for the hangman's assassinating hands. Thirdly, the scandal which it is an occasion of, for many rogues whom it teaches by public executions how one may brave dishonour and despise justice. But this charge against society requires a grave, serious investigation. I will undertake it.

36. A man is suspected, denounced, condemned

to be arrested as a murderer. Then, two, three, or more police officers are ordered out; they search, pursue, track, ensnare him on every side. At last, he is caught, chained, and brought into a jail. What becomes of him there? His mind, indeed, remains his own property, but his body is alternately made that of an attorney general, who passes it to a judge, who passes it to a jury, sitting for the purpose, and says: Here you are both accuser and accused, jurors and culprit, lawyers *pro* and *con!* Go on! I will follow. Upon your yes or no, ye jurors, my business as a judge exclusively depends. I will attend to it, as soon as yours is over. And so saying, he squares himself on his seat, passes a small elegant comb through his hair, smiles to an acquaintance, chews his quid of tobacco, or sucks some pastil, looks now and then around him, pens down a few notes, puts some questions, and waits with an indescribable coldness for his time.

37. However, the prosecution begins beneath his bench; a clerk reads the warrant; every one listens to it, and learns that the man, whom they see between two constables, who keep a watchful eye upon him, is the cause of the present meeting, and the legitimate motive of two scandalous speeches which the law approves and will soon be delivered; twelve jurors duly empanelled, set on the other side of the accused, whose face they can peruse at leisure, and whose life is now in their hands. The warrant being read, the testimony heard, the audience perfectly silent, behold another man who rises slowly from his seat, and takes a convenient place before the court! His dress is elegant, accurate, fashionable, his hair nicely combed, curled, perfumed, his smile doubtful, suspicious, sarcastic, his eye keen, alternately engaged in studying the countenance of the judge, of the jurors, of the accused, of the witnesses, of the spectators. Who is that man? A lawyer! According to the gravity of the case now pending, he has allowed his intellect to wander through the labyrinth

of a deceitful combination of subtleties, and bring forth a sequence of syllogisms, the ultimate object of which is to prove that four and four do not make eight in certain calculations, or that the sun may possibly shine by twelve at night. What a wonderful occupation!

38. Meanwhile, and in compliance with a system of opposition commanded by the law, another individual appears, whose thoughts and powers are not less marvellous, I mean the prosecuting attorney; look at him attentively, and follow well, if you can, his portentous efforts! he has levied a tax upon the measureless fields of rhetoric and metaphysics to fill up the analytical sketch of a severe philipick, and of which the thundering eloquence designs to give employment to a rope which, being tied to a beam strongly wedged in the upper part of two six or seven feet posts, shall, through his orders, and the beastly obedience of an executioner, seize the neck of a rational being and choke him to death. Listen to him, and tell me whether our poor forefathers who lived during the dark ages of a feudal tyranny, would have felt very happy if such a criminal justice as ours had honoured their time! . . . . Listen also to the testimony upon which every member of the court can exercise himself! Thanks to our system of cross-examination, judges, jurors, lawyers, prosecutors, question, as they please, the witnesses, whose answers take, of course, as many shapes and senses as there are interrogators: so it is true that the best means which we have to arrive at truth can be abused and changed into demonstrations favourable to falsehood! On the one hand, jurors who are acquainted with the law, because every good citizen makes it a duty to study the code of his own country, and who, however, are bound by the same law to judge and decide, as if they were ignorant of it, without paying attention to such feelings of mercy as nature may suggest to them;—and, on the other, a lawyer who speaks against truth legally, whose

false assertions, and, sometimes, slanders, calumnies, and scandalous wit, are publicly admired, applauded, celebrated; whilst his adversary, the prosecutor, jumps, if I can say so, at the neck of the accused, disputes him the right of saving his head, holds fast on his body, and endeavours to make of a sentence of death an oratorical ovation; like the Bengal tiger, which strikes not with his royal paw the captive traveller, but after having proudly stretched out in the sun his muscular frame and richly variegated fur. Such is the sight which our criminal courts exhibit daily! Do you not think it is beautiful, ravishing, sublime, altogether worthy of the most perfect civilization? ... But let me not speak so! It is neither ridicule nor sarcasm that will do here, but indignation, and a decided determination to mend our code.

39. Savages, ignorant of what we call better morals, get rid much quicker of their wicked fellow-wanderers. As soon as the culprit is found, they free him, instantly, by a single blow of their tomahawk, of all remorse and shame; but we, who know more than they, and boast of our improvements, we think that society is obliged to take its time with flagitiousness; we place guilt unconcernedly before us, study it at leisure, make it undergo a sort of anatomical operation, feed patiently with it our eyes, hearts and minds, and then! . . . then we give it up to shame, despair and obduracy, which will give it to a rope or a knife, which will give it to hell, very likely. No doubt we are, by so doing, above savages, but it is in cruelty!

40. The idea of a long, cruel death, associates in the mind of a savage with an idea of grandeur and courage; and this is the reason why he inflicts it upon the prisoners whom he makes in war: but contempt alone animates him when he has to deal with a vile murderer; he strikes him with a club, and all is done. Capital punishment, though it is blameable, becomes excusable with him for whom it is the mere result of immediate anger; whilst,

among us, it is a crime, so far as it is meditated, prepared and coldly executed. Hideous offspring of a calculating vengeance, it grows, I may say, amidst a thousand passions which caress it as a protector, and afterwards becomes united to our criminal justice, which we take a great care to veil before-hand, lest it should see its bloody consort. Soon, the squalid race of hanged, broken, beheaded, burnt men come out from that monstrous alliance; and nothing is so horrid to contemplate as the disgusting delivery of their infamous mother, whether it brings forth amidst the bloody preparations which surround its ill-fated couch in the public places of Europe, or in the disgraceful lurking holes in which it chooses to conceal the horrors of its infernal maternity in certain countries of America. One would say that it feasts upon its shocking barbarities, either like a shameless libertine, who sets public morals at defiance, or like a reprobated miser, who shuts himself up, far from every human eye, to eat solitarily his nauseous meal, so slow it proceeds along the plashy road which it has to go from the bench of a judge, who states upon the legitimacy of its progeny up to the scaffold, upon which this one is to receive the dreadful christening of reprobation.

41. Who has not, from time to time, entered the recesses of social vengeance? From the hangman who goes there, through a feeling of anticipation, to snuff his prey, up to the noble lord, who delights in studying the features of a far-famed murderer, all sorts of human beings crowd within the premises where a bloody contest is to take place between accusers and accused. Honest women sit often there by the lost ones; and there, also, the elegant coat of a fashionable rubs the ragged vestment of a beggar; whilst the hair richly attired of an advocate, mixes its sweet scent with the cadaverous smell which breathes out from the threatened head of his client. Indignation, fear, violence, falsehood, contempt, despair, shame, pride, humiliation, whiff over, on all

sides, their poisonous blasts across each other, and create an insufferable atmosphere, under which an obstinate curiosity sets in motion a thousand heads, which lend an anxious ear to the long-expected sentence—perhaps the sentence of death! And who is that man whose arm causes so rashly the queen of darkness to move, to raise, to threaten? Who is he? Behold him there, seated in an arm-chair! His plump and soft hands slide gently along his rosy cheeks; his look is negligently grave and solemn; worldly thoughts seem to play in his mind with legal reflections; on his lips, which now smile, and now straiten, rests the omnipotent word which will either refuse or grant the life of a man, to a slip-knot, or to a well-sharpened axe. Look at him! Feeble appears his physical strength; but his power is great. Should calumny bring you before him, and make its testimony turn against you, his hand will throw you so skilfully into those of an executioner, that you shall be dead before heaven and earth have time to come and show your innocence!

42. But, you will say: I know that man. He is a good son, a good father, a good husband, a good citizen, a righteous judge. Is he so? How comes it, then, that he may consent to be the tool, for an act of cruelty against wickedness, of sanguinary injustice against innocence? How is it? By the will of the law which dispenses him with all responsibility before men, and allows him to wash his hands in rose-water if he dips them, unwillingly, in the blood of an innocent being; or, blesses his name, and crowns his head with laurels if his sentence condemns the guilty one. The judicial carelessness of the Roman prefect, Pilate, so justly cursed by Christians, has become a rule of conduct for Christian judges. According to their doctrine, the law alone is answerable; true scapegoat, it takes with it all their wrongs. Had not the Son of Mary been God also, I doubt whether he would have foreseen that the infamous, rascally mode of admin-

istering justice followed by Pilate, was to become an approved of apology in Christian societies! But let us return to the code of nature.

43. It is not the law, but conscience which justifies man, because it is not the law which makes man, but man who makes the law. It depends upon him before he depends upon it in the natural order of things; therefore, the guilt of the law is his before all; and, if the criminal law which he claims as an excuse, offends that of nature which prohibits shedding blood, he is amenable before the superior court of reason, which condemns both the law and its author; and it is of no avail to say that the law is the work of our fathers. This circumstance impairs not the guilt; because, in the same way we are not responsible for the errors of our predecessors, so are we not excusable on account of them.

44. I cannot see but a formidable display of brutal force amidst all the scenes exhibiting in our various courts of justice. Were it not for the fear which is impressed by the weapons which the law puts into the hands of our police officers or constables, our judges would not dare to face guilt so calmly, and guilt would not tremble so cowardly before a judge. It is a real tragedy which idlers are admitted to contemplate, but which every man of sense will condemn; for whether monarchical pride or republican equality presides, its objects and effects are the same, and as reprehensible in the one case as in the other, since human nature is in both degraded, so far as the instruments of death are by both legally authorized to shed human blood, and public executioners dispense with remorse.

45. Undoubtedly, nothing is more necessary than a court of justice in society. Men, whose decayed and often misled nature is liable to so many fiendish acts, must have authorities, the business of which it shall be to countenance guilt. But such a necessity, however pressing we suppose it, has no essential connection with that gorgeous ostentation with

which, in many places, social rulers like to display their power and cause their foes to fear. It is, after all, but an exceedingly contemptible delight to appear amidst the horrors of a criminal case with a splendid dress, and like a triumphant lord, by the ladder which leads to a scaffold. To decide upon a bad action and pronounce a sentence of death, man needs not to play the part of a crazy potentate!

46. Neither do I believe that the very reprehensible practice of rendering justice democratical in its forms, can, by any means, be derived from the aforesaid necessity. A judge must not sit on the bench of Themis, as he would sit at home on a rocking chair, without any care or self respect. By walking abreast with a culprit, justice gives him a rank in society. He feels proud of it, and makes easily his mind up concerning the results of his crime, as a sentence which falls from a lip that breathes an unbecoming equality, will cause indifference but no humiliation in a guilty conscience.

47. Why not obey, in the venerable abode of the law, the impulse of nature which, in the same way as it smiles without effort when it contemplates virtue, does, without any previous arrangement, painfully shudder in presence of crime. Magistrates can neither follow a better guide, nor imitate a purer model. The dark and sombre colours with which infamy or remorse never fail to paint the malignant and sinister expression of guilty men, will suffice to inspire their judge with the imposing majesty of indignation, and the natural horror of depravity. On the stool of crime, terror, shame, despair and pride, the necessary companions of foul wickedness; conscience, which defends and accuses itself at the same time; the past lost in doing evil, the present sadly veiled with the filthy tissue of self-woven humiliation, the future which opens to show the bottomless pitch of civil reprobation:—and there, on the bench of the law, anxiety which keeps all the powers of justice mournfully awakened, doubt which tor-

ments the mind while it breaks the heart, truth that natural enemy of civil and domestic affections which so often repose upon an unsafe foundation, duty and honor the merciless adversary of every bad excuse that consideration, rank and pity may think of alleging, and, at last, society whose repose depends upon a long waited for act of public severity. Behold what nature has made to render our criminal courts grave, silent, solemn!—It is well. Let us not add any vain display to this afflictive and grievous disposition, nor impair it by a too democratical let-go!

48. I understand, likewise, that in the present state of things, force is necessary where the law is obliged to be severe. Guilty men, whosoever they be, are but madmen who, after having departed from reason violently, wander and commit depradations in society. They stand in need of a master whose look may call them back, if not to common sense, at least to a feeling of order. The keeper who is to watch over them must be something like a rational being, and use his power so that the terror he inspires may be modified by the philanthropy which guides his actions. But, if that master is a vile mercenary, and that keeper a fellow of no consideration whatever, it becomes evident that the force deputed to them, is nothing else but brutality authorized by the law. The scum of the earth is legally armed against the monsters of society, and criminal justice changed, thereby, into a tool of depravity!

49. Rousseau was right, when he said that every thing gets spoiled in the hands of man. As long as our race obeyed the wise dictates of nature, Force appeared what it is, very respectable in itself! But, as soon as we began to look at each other with a feeling of mistrust, and some dared to enter the way of evil, whilst others followed that of falsehood, Force put on the vestment of revenge, imagined tyranny, abused, in a thousand different manners, its power; and, then, society stripped of its original simplicity, was attended by maliciousness. How should we

wonder that it fell into the habit of spilling, without remorse, human blood!

50. When men are willing to retrace their steps, and bring society back to its beginning, in order to have their tribunals ruled according to the principle of family government, our judges shall cease to be a mere instrument set in motion by the law; our lawyers shall no more deny palpable facts, but discuss them candidly; jurors shall hesitate no longer between the testimony of their conscience and the sight of a scaffold; police men shall not appear like a crowd of club and pike bearers, but as the calm and respected defenders of legal order; accused men shall stand humble and dejected as it should be; and then, civil reprobation, which is the only effective chastisement that man can inflict upon man, will operate what death cannot, I mean grief, suffering, shame, regret, and, possibly, amendment. But shall we ever see that?

51. Many persons, who know nothing of our kind, except that it is such as the generality of men understand it practically, study crime no where but in books and plates, reduce misdemeanors of every sort to a number which frightens them, not because it is considerable when compared with the mass of mankind, but because those ignorant computers never went out of the narrow circle which encompasses their individuality, for which they live especially. The consequence is, that at the sight of a criminal or the report of a crime, they experience no other feelings but those of curiosity, horror, anger, and conclude, without hesitation, that a scaffold is of an absolute necessity. Murderers, they say, must be murdered! Any one who kills, must be killed! Spilled blood needs spilled blood! Nothing like retaliation! Let us have retaliation!

52. Let you have retaliation? .... How can you speak so ye vain, crazy, passionate men? Do you not see that when retaliation is become the standard of the criminal law, society shall be changed into a

den of beastly villains, and roll itself into an abyss of incurable abominations? Retaliation!... Well, let it reign and command! Your son has robbed mine, mine shall rob you! You have dishonoured my wife, I will dishonour yours! Your brother brought perdition upon my daughter, your's shall be lost through the villany of my brother! You slander your neighbour, your neighbour may slander you! You render yourself guilty of arson, we will burn your house, your barn, your harvest! And do not complain! for that is retaliation. If blood needs blood, rape needs rape, fornication needs fornication, every crime needs its like. But who can earnestly vindicate the principle of retaliation? .....

53. No one but a monster. It is the law of ill-intentioned, revengeful, anti-Christian people; it destroys at once the whole work which Jesus, the reformer of our kind, achieved on the cross; through it, we go back to those horrid times which Christian faith had in view to abolish, times of consummated wickedness, as men were, then, in the habit of repaying hatred for hatred, took eye for eye, and tooth for tooth!—*Thanks to God,* will somebody say, *we are not so bad!* I maintain that we are, for we imitate them yet in one point, which is that we ask death for death. Let us, then, cease to exact blood for blood, or confess that we are heathens whilst we continue doing so, as Christians should, in no manner, retaliate; and the true law of Christ shall not be in full vigour in our hearts, but when the very name of *executioner* has turned to be an anomaly for want of a proper use of it in our language!

54. Justice, well understood, asks not for vengeance, but for a rational punishment which, besides it works for the amendment of convicts, comprises also a due compensation for the wrongs which result from the evil suffered by the victims of a crime. Every castigation which tends not to this desirable end, is a mere act of brutality, a flagrant violation of the civil rights of man, a scandal for which the law-

giver is amenable before God and men. Now, I dare to say that, as it is practised among us, capital punishment is a direct violation of the principles of nature; and, consequently, a crime, inasmuch as it defrauds both the culprit and the victim of their natural rights. That demands a further explanation.

55. Any man whom the law arraigns as a murderer, is such, either through a contingency, in consequence of an unaccountable predisposition to crime, or in virtue of a horrible necessity, which is determined either by a free indulgence of bad habits, or a criminal mode of living which he has chosen. In the first instance, his crime is but a simple transgression, which becomes the only object to be attained or punished by the law, in order that a due and proper commutation be accomplished. In the second instance, his crime results from a defect in his organization; and, therefore, a cell in a lunatic asylum is the only remedy to be used for the purpose of hindering him from doing evil, and securing society against his foul deeds. In the third instance, the general interest or welfare of the community unites with the individual whom his crime has injured directly; then, besides the punishment inflicted for the sake of that individuality, the culprit should suffer another which may satisfy the community, and put him beyond the possibility of offending it again. Let us understand well these principles of justice!

56. A murder has been committed through hatred, vengeance, covetousness, misguided love, passionate jealousy, or any other private motive which the position of the murderer towards his victim has determined; that is what I call a private act, as it is evident that in any other circumstance, or in relation with any other person, there would have been no murder. Now, I contend that in this case, the interest of those who suffer by the crime, and not that of the community, should be taken mainly into consideration, and the punishment inflicted accordingly.

The convict should thus be told: "You have killed! your unruly passion led you to murder! that is a crime for which you must both atone and account. The court, considering that a man whose passions are so ungovernable as to cause him, in their cruel fits, to kill and spill blood, is dangerous in a community, it condemns you, therefore, to prison for life, lest some other member of the said community be killed by you, should a similar case occur.

57. "But, also, whereas the person whom you have killed had his worldly interests, which you have hurt materially, and obligations to fulfil, which you have disabled him to attend to, it is a justice due and ordered by this court, that you should compensate the said interests, and, inasmuch as possible, accomplish the said obligations. Whom have you killed? The father of a family, left destitute in consequence of his untimely death;—a young man, a girl, upon whose exertions depended the living of the unfortunate ones whom the death of your victim afflicts and throws into deep misery! You shall be forced to work during your captivity, and the produce of your labour shall be given to them. Is it, on the contrary, a man or a woman of wealth, whose existence you have thus so cruelly put an end to? The law, in this case, abides by the presumption that wealthy people, being the natural supporters of the poor, should give them alms; and, without changing your punishment, orders that all that you earn shall be set at the disposal of the guardians of the poor."

58. This punishment, I say, would be rational, and agree perfectly with the spirit of commutation which every law must have in view, as adequate. William Penn, the founder of the state of Pennsylvania, in North America, understood that it should be so; and such would have been his legislation if it had depended exclusively upon him. But men like him are very scarce! Why has it been decided that, in the actual state of society, such a commutation

should be dispensed with? Because society, fallen as it is in the abyss of egotism, obeys its passions, and not truth; thinks it more convenient to have revenge, like a tyrant, than to comply with a sacred duty, like an honest man. In its hands, judges are mere bodies, the minds and hearts of which it condemns to silence, that it may use them, without difficulty, as means of satisfying its cruelties. Materialist in its acts, it endeavours to justify them by the pretended morality of its laws. The victims who suffer in consequence of a murder, are in its eyes a motive of barbarity, and that is all. It starts from their misfortune to authorize its judicial murders, and leaves no other consolation to their grief, no other compensation to the wrongs which they endure, but the sight of a scaffold and a cursed grave in which putrefaction and worms are gnawing the cause of both its cruelties and injustice. Humanity complains, I believe, of this system: but few men admire it, and civilization is bound to thank them for it. Poor human race!

59. Whenever I consult the criminal records of nations, I see that, upon a moderate average, the number of crimes varies but little in comparison with populations. It seems that depravity, like the breakers of a stormy sea, has received, from a benevolent and attentive God, the order never to pass certain limits: but, on another side, I perceive, that whilst God watches over society as a good father, society watches over its subjects as a tyrant. It seems that it progresses only to be less philanthropic than before, though it boasts of its being much more so. In proportion as it tramples upon the rights of those who are injured by a murder, abandons and discards them altogether, it increases the income of sheriffs, jailers, and executioners, whose profession is the more and the more benefitted by the materialism of the law. Indeed, it is scandalous! Let us go back to the principle.

60. Some persons acquainted with the researches

made by me with regard to this sort of punishment, have asked what I would do with parricides. I never gave, nor will ever give to this question another answer but the statements which I have proposed above. Parricides are murderers whose punishment should be directed by the same laws and motives which decide upon the condition of a common homicide. The intensity or extent of a crime is less the object of the law than the castigation of it as a foul deed which society must condemn. Besides, I see, in a father who kills his son, a son who murders his father, mother, or brother, a brother who stabs his sister, a sister who chokes her brother, a mother who smothers her child, but stupendous monsters who must be chained in a deep, dark cell, unless they are maniacs, and deserve to be treated as such.

61. Whatever arguments one may bring against the custom which prevails of pleading monomania in the criminal courts, it is certain that this sort of insanity exists among men. I have known some who were actually devoured with a horrible thirst for human blood, and panted after it, like tigers in the wilderness. I have seen others who would pass silently at night into a grave-yard, there to take out bodies from their coffins, feast with worms on half rotten bowels, and suck voluptuously what blood was left in putrified veins:—An example among many, will show how far in the way of crime, those unfortunate *Hemodipsites* can go.

62. " A young woman born of poor parents, entered, when seventeen years of age, the service of a rich countryman, whose farm laid in the neighbourhood. Ordered by her master to attend at the table, she let the desire of partaking of all the dainties which she handed to others, prey upon her gradually. As desire is more a defect than a crime, she did not take much pains in resisting it. The effects of this negligence, however, proved soon to be unconquerable. Her morbid imagination, daily excited by her gluttony, went so far as to represent, in forms which

no pencil can depict, the supernatural results those delicious viands would cause in the human body, which seemed, piece by piece, to whet the epicurean appetite of all the family in which she was but an humble servant. She thought, during those moments of a greedy exultation, that she saw the blood and fat of a rich, well-prepared roast, mixing with the delicate blood and tenderly fed flesh of the guests, their soft and almost transparent skin kept alive and seducing by the superior merit of a nicely seasoned chicken, or matchless delicacy of reed birds. A sort of intoxicating perfume, made out of the breath of man, and the odour of animal food blending together, pervaded all her senses, whenever she moved around the privileged company whose dainties she could not share; and her longing appetite, stirred up to madness by that imaginary scent, would whet desperately her teeth which poverty ordered to be dull. Often had she bitten, in her accesses of gluttonous fury, the tender limbs of a child confided to her care! Often had she, during the momentary absence of the scullion, sucked the blood of such animals as were destined to supply the table! The first drops of this horrible drink, she had been, at first, unable to swallow. Much cruel remorse, too, had raged in her mind, when she first attempted biting the flesh of a living child. But what has a bad habit not overcome?—what can it not effect upon our frail and wretched kind? That which had inspired her with horror soon seemed to her like a very natural sensation. She changed a criminal propensity into a justifiable want, and, step after step, she fell into an abyss from which she never returned. Just like a girl, whose virtue has been once lost, falls into all the disorders of life, she abandoned herself to her wretched passion and thirst for human blood. Indeed, it was such that no remorse, no fear could restrain it. She answered the last reproach of her conscience, as a libertine, sold to infamy, answers the pungent censures of his, that is to say, in satisfying the more and the more every day, a passion which had, by dint of being indulged, grown uncontrollable. The sight of a child excited in her that ravenous desire which the presence of a lad produces in the degraded mind of a prostitute, or the arrival of a rich traveller produces in that of a bloody highway robber.

"But will ever as feeble an intellect, as that of man's, be able to describe all the thoughts and feelings which must have fought with each other in the conscience of a woman thus preparing for an ignominious death? Phrenologists, philosophers, and all the wise who think they know mankind, would find themselves at a loss here, and be obliged to acknowledge how imperfect and vain our views of human nature may often be. Heaven itself, had it not the key to all secrets, would be thunderstruck in presence of such monsters, and doubt its power over the incomprehensible beings who seem to dishonour, thus, its wisdom.

"The priest, to whom in a moment of despair, they consent to reveal all that passes in their minds, hearts and bodies, cannot help trembling. He looks and listens attentively, but, at the same time, doubts the testimony of his senses, invokes the light of God, and questions the possibility of such horrors.

"Can this be a human being, who stands now by me, and accuses himself of crimes unknown? Or, is it one of Lucifer's companions, whose irons have been broken for a time, and now attempts to mock here the holy ministry of Christian faith and hope? Shall I call to my help the prayers of the church, and a special inspiration of the Holy Ghost, or those chains of iron which secure madness in its last asylum? Will I invoke the terrors of religion or police officers?

"So thought the clergyman to whom that unhappy woman communicated the horrible state of her conscience! He told me, himself, that such was the distracted condition into which he fell on hearing the disclosures made by her, that any person who would have seen him then, would have certainly believed, that he was an accomplice of the crime revealed to him.

" A mortal paleness, added he, veiled my frightened face; a cold sweat fell along my shaking limbs: the words of heaven, which I tried to recollect, breathed slow, anxious, almost unheard, on my parched lips; and the silence of death, awful fortuneteller of any one who consults it, prevailed, at last, in my room, where I had never held before but pious conversations with my Christian brethren, but in which, then, a guilty, incorrigible person struck his pastor with a dreadful fear, and disconcerted him by the calm, cold, indifferent narration of his horrible propensities.

"I shuddered at these remarks, and looked terrified.

" What do you think I did, asked the clergyman, when I found myself in such a predicament?

" Indeed, reverend sir, I know not! replied I.

" Well! continued he,—I raised my eyes to God! I asked him whether he had allowed a single feeling of religion to remain in that soul, redeemed with the blood of His Son, and said; if Thou wilt grant such a feeling, oh, my good Lord! I answer for its salvation, I will move, I will frighten, I will touch it! Alas! this very feeling which, in my opinion, should have saved it, was the cause of its loss. Faith created in the powers of that wretched creature, the devouring effect of oil on fire. The more the voice of God endeavoured to enter sweet, persuasive and powerful, in her, the more did her passion inflame itself, and get irritated. It opposed despair to shame, violence to remorse, the thirst of blood to the regret of wishing for it. So, after many struggles, in which virtue was overpowered, that poor girl, whirled by her monomania from abyss into abyss, freed herself from my charitable hands, which tried to keep her back, and fell into those of crime which soon hurled her into those dark, horrid cells, where the justice of scaffolds keeps its victims.

"Young, as I said, handsome, noble looking, strong and courageous, she prefers, among the various sorts of glory which life offers her sex, the triumph of an ignominious death. But this preference, mind me, springs in her from one of those ever to be dreaded necessities of which God alone can give a correct account.

"Cursed be," she exclaimed in the first access of a frightful inspiration, "the bosom which brought me forth! Cursed be the man who gave me life, and with it the right of being wicked, cruel, and a drinker of blood! Curses and death on all the children whom the union of my father and mother has allowed to make their appearance on earth! Perhaps the thirst which devours me, will devour them also! If I allow them to live, our family will continue but to generate monsters like me! Let them all die then! Let my hand kill all of them, and secure, thus, the tranquillity of our neighbours!

"So she spoke, after having left her pastor whom alone she revered and feared; and soon did her deeds agree horribly with her words! Her father, mother, and two of her sisters fell dead, within their native cottage, under the blows of an axe whetted by her for the purpose, and the power of which was increased by her reckless passion. Streams of blood run by her; she sees it, wonders at it, but smiles on it, and keeps awfully calm amidst the panting ruins of a slaughter which should frighten her mind, tear it to death, and heave up the rage of despair in its most secret parts. All the neighbours are attracted to the spot by the cries of a little boy, her brother, whom she missed, whilst her fury aimed, before all, at the life of her father; they stand at a distance, no one dares to approach her, the fatal axe is still in her hands, she brandishes it over the bodies of her victims, like a conqueror his sword over the field of battle; she leans on it as if it was a sceptre, and seems to challenge the witnesses of her crime, and to command their fate. At last, however, her passion sinks, her anger and violence cease, she lets the axe fall, gives herself up to the officers of justice, bends before the destiny which she has provoked, but which she ceases not to brave.

"I need not tell with what feelings of horror the news of her sanguinary deed was heard of throughout the world around; with what imprecations, curses, cries of vengeance she was accompanied to her dungeon; how terrific the day of her trial; how the minds and the hearts of all those present felt deeply impressed, nay, freed from every fear, filled with content, when sentence of death was passed upon her; how solemn was her execution!

"But, I must say, that amidst the universal reprobation of which she became the victim, she never gave up the afflicting and horribly mysterious calmness with which she had committed a parricide unparalleled in the annals of crime, and set at defiance the horrors of infamy. She never answered her accusers and judges but with the inculpating silence of guilt; felt neither shame before men whom she feared not, nor remorse in her heart, which, as if unconscious of her sad and dreadful position, she seemed to have hardened in iniquity. The sight of the executioner inspired her with an inconceivable joy; her lips betrayed a smile, when her eyes did, at last, rest upon the scaffold; she prayed to heaven, where she hoped to enter, and have, very soon, a sweet repose; sneered at this earth, which she left without pain; and expressed, before her death, but a single regret, that of leaving a younger brother, whom, said she to her pastor, a salutary blow of her axe would have dispensed with the horrible necessity of eating human flesh, and of dying with his unsatisfied thirst of blood amidst the humiliations of an execution."

63. Now, reader, come to the scaffold of that un-

happy girl! Look at it, for your imagination can now see it easily, and tell me: Did she deserve to perish upon it?—All those who witnessed her crime and judged of its enormity, after the legal testimony which established her guilt, thought that she did; nay, they said that strangling or beheading was for such a wicked one a punishment too mild.—But one man who had known her long, before she was made guilty by the law, and by the law thrown into the sink of justice, excused her in his conscience, and was saying to himself as he came back from the place of execution: "Not there, but in a lunatic asylum should she have ceased to live!"—That man was her pastor. I think that he alone was right!

64. We laymen can hardly understand how many and how deep the mysteries of our nature are. It is but when conscience consents to unfold its secrets that the recesses of all our miseries, faults and defects can be well seen, measured, registered. Then only can we comprehend fully the true effects of that inward struggle, which both the good which speaks in the name of God, and evil which comes from the foe of our race, keep constantly alive within us. Many persons who seem to be very wicked are very often not so, and, very often too, we think that those people are honest who are indeed very criminal. Crime like virtue is nothing very great, if we look only at their outside forms and effects. To make of them an object of either hatred or admiration, we need to know well and positively all the motives which precede them, and all the accidents which qualify them in a human being. But who shall ever possess that science? No one but a minister of the gospel, who, though he is obliged to keep what faults he knows very secret, cannot, however, help seeing all that human nature is capable of in its hours of aberration, and may, for the instruction of men, make a discreet use of an experience so much more certain as it is founded upon evident facts, thoughts and feelings.

65. Before I undertook to examine the question now pending, I consulted, also, several Catholic clergymen about it. All confirmed, by their testimony, the opinion of the Protestant minister which I have mentioned above, and I believed that, consequently, it must be altogether correct, for all that which they know, through their holy ministry, of human miseries and foibles, is, by far, of a greater extent and more accurate than all that other men can comprehend and even imagine of the same subject. Whatever may our efforts be to approach and penetrate the secret laboratories of crime, we can hardly see it but by the light of a philosophical inquiry and mathematical combination, whilst those gentlemen have, through auricular confession, a fair opportunity to seize all the details, particulars, appendices and shades of depravity. With his fellow laymen every one will avow such faults as are daily committed by others, nay, boast of them; but it is to a Catholic priest only that he will consent to reveal all the petty and shameful circumstances which have accompanied them. Man is very often proud of a sin, but blushes at the very thought of his foibles, which he would not let be known for the world.—Why? Because we are willing to acknowledge what may flatter our vanity, and anxious to conceal what may make us pass either for a libertine or a wicked person, in the way men are pleased to understand libertinism and wickedness. So is it with theft, hatred, vengeance, seduction, adultery, murder! A man guilty of any of these crimes will, possibly, recognise that he has committed the act, when he is brought before a court, or in presence of men, but he will always keep for the priest, supposing he believes in confession, all such accounts as may either aggravate or diminish his guilt.

66. From this undeniable fact, I conclude that this is a rather scandalous law, which makes it a duty for jurors, in our criminal courts, never to view but the guilt as it results from the testimony. The judge

being, then, a mere organ of another law, which orders him never to see any thing else but what sentence is applicable to the case as it is decided by the jurors, it follows from this legal combination, that morality, properly so called, is, practically, excluded from our judicial councils; for if the jurors, notwithstanding every prohibition intimated by the code, were not sometimes obstinate upon the natural right which they have of calculating the results as much as the subject of their verdict; and if some judges, in spite of the text which dispenses them with yielding to a feeling of mercy, did not, occasionally, try their best to impair the intended effects of the testimony, our criminal courts, however necessary they are, would be a mere ambush or snare laid by the law, in the way of crime, to catch it first, and then chastise it, no matter how. So the African hunters do, when they chase the ferocious beasts of the wilderness; but civilized nations might, I think, be a little more humane when they deal with crime, and grant something to the intention of the accused!

67. It is true, that the case in which I chose to demonstrate the possibility of monomania, and its extraordinary effects in some individuals, presents a very peculiar character which places it far above the habitual powers of human understanding. It is a sort of monstrous prodigy; but it tends, nevertheless, to show that this defect is not, possibly, so rare as one might suppose. If I exhibited one of its most horrible consequences, it was in order to have the lesser ones more easily admitted. Religious and political fanaticism are, most assuredly, monomanias. It is a crime to shed the blood of man for the purpose of either honouring God or supporting a system. However, religious pyres and political scaffolds never were considered but lamentable follies, directed by dangerous convictions. But if religion and politics can decide man to commit murder, why could it not be so with another passion? Religion and politics are, indeed, but two very small fractions of human fanaticism!

68. The protest entered against monomania, considered as a plausible motive of excuse before a criminal court, is grounded upon this fact, that no murderer could exist whose lawyer would not invoke in his favour this infirmity of our nature; and that thus, crime should always avoid a due punishment. I will answer, that monomania, though it is a very admissible apology, cannot, however, be a full justification. As soon as it has become so dangerous as to prove fatal either to individuals or to society, it must be restrained; and it is the duty of our magistrates to take such means as will be judged necessary to impede efficaciously its bloody deeds. So, no other risk shall be run, in the case we admit monomania as an excuse, but that of having no more any use for scaffolds and gallows. Besides, that risk would be rather a profit than a disadvantage to society, so far as it is of a higher morality to be less cruel towards a criminal, than to expose justice to inflict death upon a poor, unfortunate, insane man. Imprisonment is, at any rate, a severe punishment, when it is not a remedy.

69. When this mode of correction is adopted exclusively, few criminals will escape it. The possibility which it leaves to judges of retracing their steps, and mastering, at all times, the effect of their sentence, will save them from an excessively dangerous hesitation with regard to the punishment of crimes. Many villains who escape death, thanks to a feeling of fear or pity on the part of a juror, should otherwise, be duly punished. The sight of a dungeon appears not like a scaffold in the eyes of a scrupulous citizen upon whose judgment depends the fate of a fellow being. Many jurors, who decline loading their conscience with their consent to a judicial murder, would not hesitate returning a verdict, the only effect of which should be to secure guilt in a solitary cell. However horrible the sufferings ordered in that cell may be, it has but an indirect power over its subject, and can, at any time, be

forced to render him back to liberty and honour, if his innocence is established, whilst death never can return the victims immolated on its block. This is a remark which, I think, should be taken into a serious consideration.

70. On another side, the judgments of men are not always founded upon an absolute certainty. Many circumstances which do apparently concur to give to falsehood the very shades of truth, deceive the most acute minds, and bring legally into question the cause of innocence. It is, unhappily, too true, that virtue has more than once been confounded with vice, and given up, in consequence of an unjust sentence, to that shame and those chastisements which were intended for guilt only. I know two examples of this deplorable error; the one which I borrow from the registers of a jail, and the other from the annals of a scaffold. I will relate them.

71. "Some twenty or thirty years ago, a young clergyman, a member of the far and justly celebrated society of Saint Sulpice of Paris, went to spend his holydays in his birthplace. Informed of his arrival, the chaplain of the prison there, availed himself of the good will of his colleague in the holy ministry, and left him for a few months, the care of his incarcerated flock, whilst he himself spent that time in his own family.

"Immediately after he was gone, the Sulpitian, whose mind was pleased to interrogate humanity in any stage of virtue or vice in which it would present itself to him, began his new ministry. It was, indeed, new for him, and often was he frightened when depravity consented to acquaint him with its impure conceptions. However, Providence ordained that, among the unexpected orders of penitents who were so different from those pious students, whose conscience he was accustomed to guide in the practice of virtue, he met with one whose fate interested his pity. It was a man whom he supposed to be something like forty years of age. During a period of ten years, which had elapsed since the day on which he was committed, that man had learned, by dint of grief and resignation, how to master all his motions and gestures, and would submit, without murmuring, to privations of all kinds, suffer humiliations from any person who came, apply himself, faithfully, to any sort of hard labour which the jailer was pleased to impose upon him. His look was calm though deeply sad, his face quite pale, and his body very thin, not only for want of proper food, but also in consequence of the inward afflictions which preyed upon his mind. His fellow prisoners liked and respected him; the jailguards spoke well of him; the sisters of charity had often admired his exemplary conduct, and praised his astonishing moderation and patience. He would not entertain the inmates of the prison nor any visiter with the history of his grief and sufferings, but was satisfied with protesting modestly in favour of his innocence, shedding a few tears, raising his eyes to heaven, and crossing himself piously. That done, he would return to his habitual silence and recollections.

"Indeed, circumstances so mysterious should have drawn the attention of his jailer and judges!—it was not so, however; on the contrary, the directors of the prison, guided, exclusively, in their opinion by the statements recorded in the jail book, never saw in him but a villain justly sentenced to twenty years of hard labour. The chaplain himself, deceived, I suppose, by an error of judgment, alas! too common even among clergymen, had always considered him as a dangerous, studied hypocrite. Only a sister of charity, who used to see him oftener, and approach him nearer, felt disposed to pity him sincerely, and believed that he was innocent; but, she dared not to insist upon her opinion, as every body else would contradict it, unless one had referred the matter to that of the other convicts, who, all, agreed upon the injustice which persecuted thus their fellow sufferer.

"On whatever side he would look, his eyes always met with jailers or foes. Days passed for him, filled with bitter thoughts and painful feelings. No hope of seeing those to come bettered in any way, had entered his dejected soul. God, whom he had invoked at first, and begged for his release, had not come to his help in the manner as he thought this only consoler of man would. Distressed in his heart, but strong in his faith, he did not murmur for that, but respected the silence of his heavenly Master, considered himself as a creature whom the eternal wisdom had judged proper to abandon to sufferings on earth, and he bent with a pious resignation under the rod of chastisement, persuaded that all was for the best.

"Then, all the mysteries of Job, the Arabian patriarch, were renewed in a dungeon. The prisoner embraced misery and shame, civil reprobation, and prison toils, as if they had been sent to him by Providence as the means of salvation. His soul, inspired by the true spirit of our Christian gospel, rose as high as the cross of his Saviour Jesus, in proportion as his body, delivered up to excruciating pains, bowed towards a despised grave, of which his miserable couch and rotten straw were the desolating image.

"There he was, a prey to his last trial, when the young priest visited him for the first time. On being so unexpectedly offered words of consolation to which his ears were hardly accustomed, he raised slowly his head, and exclaimed: My father! God bless you! you are just in time to see a dying man!—have pity on me!—help me to reconcile myself with my Creator, and leave this vale of tears with a sincere hope of being welcomed in heaven!

The clergyman, as he heard these words inspired by a deep grief, was much moved. He thought that repentance had worked happily in the prisoner's soul. He thanked God for this unexpected grace, approached nearer the couch of the dying man, and exhorted him to do penance for his sins. Alas! my father! replied the penitent, I have been here a prisoner, ten long and painful years; if God deigns to accept them as a due penance, I will think that my sufferings were a favour from him, and die content, very content; you may believe it, my father! It is well, my son, answered the priest. Truth, I see, has enlightened your mind;—the recollections of virtue touch you, and revive your heart; your regret will no doubt render you excusable; confess now your sins and they will be forgiven; the cross of Jesus, by which you are about to breathe your last, will prove to be profitable to your misguided soul, and the blood of our good Saviour, like a beneficent dew from above, will renew its youth, and render it worthy of heaven.

"In saying so, he sat by his penitent, to whom he lent a favourable ear, though he was prepared for hearing a long, sad history of a life polluted by many crimes. But, how great and deep-felt was his astonishment, when, after the avowals of the prisoner, he found that he stood by one of those honest and innocent souls which the blast of evil cannot wither, and in which the Spirit of God is pleased to dwell, there to show how vain are the efforts of the wretched tempter of our nature, when man obeys the will of heaven. At first, he doubted, fearing that his penitent concealed the truth, like Ananias at the feet of Peter, and reprehending him mildly, added: My son! think of your present condition! Death stands at your door; it knocks, it opens, it enters; it preys upon you in this place where men, permit me to say, did not immure you on account of your virtues! True, my father! but you may believe me, I am not here for my crimes! I am innocent! I suffer unjustly; God knows it! Bless me, my father, bless me! .... And he burst into tears: he sobbed profoundly as a saint who falls on his knees, seeking consolation in his faith to a God whose great sufferings are the only protection of persecuted innocence.

"The scene was touching, solemn, heart-rending. The words of the priest breathed unuttered on his lips, and fell back on his tender, pure, sensible, merciful mind; his hand trembled as he stretched it over the prisoner's head, to let the graces of a well-merited absolution drop sweet and vivifying into an honest heart. He believed now that his penitent was punished unjustly by men, and severely tried by God; and when he saw that this poor soul, which human justice had endeavoured to degrade, was breaking its earthly ties, to start spotless for heaven, he exclaimed: Behold! O God of mercy! here calumny has brought and abandoned thy servant! Crime may enjoy now its own work, and prey upon the body of its victim! but thou, Christian soul! long enough have been thy trials! Go! enter thy rest and glory! Go, and mix thy voice with the hymns of angels! Go, and pray . . . for thy confessor! pray! . . . . .

"He could say no more. Abundant tears flowed over his burning cheeks; he knelt; a still, profound, heavenly calmness reigned in the cell; the solemn whispers of Eden alone broke softly through the religious silence which had prevailed. He thought he saw the soul of the deceased enter the blissful regions above, and let, as if inspired by triumphing truth, these cheering words start from his chaste heart: All now is done!—the saint is dead!

"Dead! exclaimed from without all the prisoners whom curiosity had assembled around the cell!—Dead! . . . . And the priest saw them hurrying to the ragged vestments which the deceased wore. Each of these remains of a despised poverty was by them torn to pieces religiously, and each piece carried away like a precious relic.

"Then, the jailers, astonished and moved by such a pious commotion and manifestation of a wonderful respect to an unknown, unpitied captive, began to conceive some doubts with regard to the guilt of the dead. The attorney general was informed of all. He ordered new inquiries; they were made—but in vain; the secret laid in the conscience of a single man whom his like could not penetrate. Religion alone, which had blessed the innocent, could find, with a pardon in its hands, the guilty,—and it found him!

"Two years had elapsed, when the same clergyman was visited, at the country-seat of a gentleman, his friend, by the curate of a neighbouring village, and begged by him to call at one of his parishioners', who now, on his death-bed desired, his presence. To hear the message, and comply with the wishes of the bearer, was for the Sulpitian but the work of an instant. He goes, he enters, he approaches a labourer whom despair agitates on his bed: a sudden recollection of the prison scene awakes in his mind; he speaks, he questions the sick man; he discovers the truth which he had so long desired to know:—a written acknowledgment and confession of the crime for which the poor prisoner had suffered, is handed to him by the labourer, who was guilty of it, but had waited the hour of his death to reinstate innocence."

70. The other example is still more afflicting. "A grenadier of the old imperial guard in France, was returning home gaily after the long and toilsome campaigns of Napoleon. Sure that he would find, at every place where every travelling soldier has a right to stop, both his pittance and a shelter, he let his sabre keep time behind him as he went his way quietly; his knapsack seemed light on his erect shoulders; he smiled on every young man or girl, and bowed respectfully to every old man or woman whom he met along the road; he sang, alternately, the souvenirs of glorious days at Austerlitz and Marengo, the lofty pyramids of Egypt, the battle fields of Spain and Austria, the plains of Rus-

sia, with their storms of snow, icy routes, and fatal sky; in a word, the whole history of the French empire followed, sad but glorious, his well and lightly measured steps. Who would have thought that, happy as he looked, he was actually walking to a scaffold; he, I say, who was as brave as his sword was sharp, as simple as a child, as quiet as an old man, as pure and as honest as the very soul of the old guard? There it was, however, that he went, though unaware of it; and circumstances combined, it seems, to bring him there.

"Arrived at a small town in which he was allowed to ask for a lodging, he passes his sunburnt hand over his gray moustaches, enters the mayor's office, obtains a quartering billet, and, with it, goes to the house which had been indicated to him. The landlord, unable to receive him, sends him to an adjoining tavern, with a written promise to pay for his expenses. The grenadier, accustomed as he was to take and use life as it came, accepts the order, goes straight to the tavern, whose keeper welcomes him eagerly, and calls him, soon, to supper.

"The table was frugal but good. A horse dealer, just arrived from a fair, where he had exchanged his horses for round, sounding silver pieces, which he caused to clang gently in his waist pocket, by shaking it, as a dandy would his watch-guard, sat there with him.

"I see," said the grenadier abruptly, "your trade is more profitable than mine."

"So I think," replied the horse dealer.

"I am glad you are satisfied with it, but I do not envy you, thanks to God!"

"Most likely; for you, glory is, I suppose, preferable to wealth."

"Yes, on a field of battle; but in a tavern, wealth is better."

"Perhaps you want money? Here, I have plenty of it at your service, my dear fellow."

"Thank you, my friend! thank you! a quartering

billet is enough for the present; when I have entered civil life again, I will work also, and, in spite of old nick, my toils, I hope, will bring money in my purse."

"Well said, Grenadier! Please, where are you going now?"

"I am going home; that is to say at N. . . ."

"N. . . . I know that place: I have friends in the neighbourhood of it; often have I transacted business with them; it is likely we shall meet again there."

"I hope we shall! Come, good friend, and may the blade of this, my sabre, pierce me through and through, if I do not drown you in a cask of good wine!"

"Do you sleep here to night?"

"Yes, I do."

"So much the worse, I am bound to travel alone; but it would have made me happy to go on, side by side with you."

"Ah! ah! I understand my good man! You carry some cash with you, and you say, should the old guard follow, all is safe! Well, well, I will follow. Hallo! the house here!"

"Here I am," answered the landlord, "what is the matter?"

"I wish to know what you charge for a bed?" inquired the grenadier.

"Thirty cents."

"Thirty cents!—I will waste them in wine. Bring another bottle of it! My friend here will drink a few glasses more with me, and off I go with him afterwards."

"This fatal bargain being accepted by the horse-dealer, the two guests went on, toasting each other, until midnight.—Then, they started, arm in arm, helping one another along, describing here and there figures of every imaginary shape, singing with a friendly competition, setting kings and bishops at defiance, mastering the whole world which neither of them knew as it is;—and so would they have spent the rest of the night if fate, unaccountable fate, had not ordered, for the misfortune of the grenadier, that they should separate.

"As they passed by a lane which opened at a right angle to the high road, and went, winding above, between hills planted with vine and trees, the horse-dealer stopped, thought of some other business which the wine had caused him to forget, and told his companion, that in spite of the pleasure which he would enjoy by following him, he was obliged to take the lane and go to a place where he was waited for, promised to meet him on the next day at the first town, shook hands with him heartily, and disappeared among the hills.

"The grenadier always ready, I have said, to put up with circumstances, bids him a last farewell, shrugs up his shoulders to set his knapsack right again, tries with a good stroke on the ground the strength of his stick, looks front, commands to march, and begins anew his solitary journey, which he endeavoured to make gayer by resuming his favourite airs.

"He had just began to sing, when a hungry wolf, which was roving along the road in search of prey, howled with a threatening ferocity, rushed on him, and would have torn him to pieces, had not the grenadier quickly moved back and skilfully avoided him, drawing in the meantime his sabre from the scabbard, and piercing the animal through with the happiest dexterity.

"The wolf, then, feeling its strength impaired by the wound which it had received, yelled horribly, and ran for shelter into a thick wood, where its carcass was looked for in vain afterwards.

"Its painful moans caused, at first, the traveller to tremble, and dark dreadful thoughts passed through his mind; but, proud of his speedy triumph, he soon dissipates them, sheathes carelessly his weapon yet tinged with blood, sends all the wolves to the Cossacks, and goes on as merrily as before.

"The horse-dealer, meanwhile, had followed silently the way which he had chosen, unfortunately for him. The moon had disappeared, and the dense foliage of two rows of trees, the branches of which crossed each other over the road, made it darker, or, at least, more perilous for the traveller whose destiny had brought him there. He was hardly one mile off when two ruffians jumped suddenly from behind a thick hedge across his path, seized him by the throat, stifled his voice, stabbed him to the heart, robbed him of his money, and threw his body into a deep ditch by the road side.

" Had the grenadier gone his way, no suspicions, at least no proof to accuse him would have been found; but, feeling uneasy for his new made friend, on account of the money which he knew he had, and fearing some bad encounter for him, he decided to retrace his steps and rejoin him. As soon thought, as soon done, and back he goes up to the entrance of the lane; recognises it well, follows its trodden path hastily, calling loudly, from time to time, after the horse-dealer; but, alas! a dreadful silence answers him. Alone he goes, and arrives at the village of * * *

" It was sunrise. The people, early risers there, were leaving their cottages to go to their daily labours. They see the soldier, look at him attentively, remark his anxious, fatigued, worn out countenance, whilst he questions them about his friend. No body had seen him. Well, said the grenadier, that is a proof that he walks well. He is like me, a merry Andrew. He carries wine, too, as well as a trooper. God bless his legs! it is only one league more that I have to run. And so saying, he turned towards another road which led to the town where he hoped to meet with the horse dealer, and make with him another good repast.

"The poor fellow! He had hardly stepped into the town hall and asked for a lodging, when the men-of-arms seized him, dragged him to jail like a villain, threw him into a dungeon, and left him alone with his uncollected thoughts. He wandered, at first, from one idea to another; but soon felt something like a suspicion. He calls for the jailer, interrogates him, and endeavours to ascertain the motive of his arrest. All he suspected is true. His friend had been murdered. He passes for the murderer. Shame, dishonour, death await him!

"On the day of his trial, judges, accusers, witnesses, spectators, all agree in believing him guilty. It is in vain that he pleads not guilty and protests his innocence. He tells them candidly all the circumstances as they were, save that of the murder, which he knows not how to account for, but they believe him not. The testimony of the tavern keeper and of the villagers of * * *, and, more especially, the blood with which his sabre was tinged, are considered as a sufficient proof of his guilt. Mercy, pity, God, all abandon him. His head, cut by the hand of an executioner, rolls on a scaffold. His cursed remains are sent to the worms in an unhallowed spot. His name is disgraced before the world.—Unhappy man! But unhappier still are the judges and jurors! Truth will soon come forth to fill their consciences with sadness and remorse!

"Not long after, the same court, and eight of the same jurors were sitting within the same premises to decide upon the fate of two villains, who had to atone, at last, for their many crimes, and clear the grenadier by their confession.

"As they were, one day, gambling in a remote room of a tavern, and overheated by the liquor which they had drunk freely, they began to quarrel and reproach each other for the murder of the horse dealer. Some bystanders hear them. Justice is in-informed,—they are arrested,—their life is investigated, their guilt established beyond a doubt, though they persist in denying it. As long as hope breathes in them, they lament their fate, they protest, they pray; but at the sight of the executioner, in presence of the people, on the scaffold, before they fall into eternity, they raise their voice, they confess their crime; and the grenadier is justified on the same spot where he had suffered; his fame is restored; no murderer ever came out from the old guard, thank heaven!"

May now the earth lay lightly on his mangled body! May the flowers of innocence grow luxuriant, and bloom ever fresh over his forsaken grave! But let also his lamentable fate instruct judges and jurors of all countries. The number of the innocent men thus killed judicially, is not so small as it is believed generally.

73. Thus, insanity on the one part, and, on the other, the possibility of confounding innocence with guilt, and, besides, that which a well organized society owes to those persons, who suffer in consequence of a murder committed upon a being, whose life was necessary to them, are as many conclusive motives which should decide in favour of the abolition of capital punishment by modern nations, and impel them to reimplace it by a lunatic asylum for the first, and solitary confinement or hard labour for the others.

74. The objection drawn from the practical consent and tradition of all nations to oppose this important reformation of our criminal codes, is, by no means decisive, when we compare it with the strong and momentous arguments which militate in favour of the adverse principle which is altogether more prudent, and thereby, more rational. The time in which we live, a time of social improvement, and in which men seem to be willing to rise to the highest perfection that can be reached by them, tells us that we have less occasion to know what past societies ordered, or what some modern people want to order, than to determine what is to be done for the

best interest of all in a community where reason prevails a little more than it does elsewhere. There is for us no obligation whatever to respect such laws or customs of our predecessors as cannot harmonize with the present religious and political developement of society. Every thing is doomed to change among men. What was true, several thousand years ago, ceased to be so after the triumph of Christianity over Mythology. Many doctrines, also, which the former pontiffs and preachers of Christianity taught as uncontrovertible, were ranged, by their successors, among those false, incomplete, superstitious notions which, let it be said to our shame, do, from time to time, pervade and master our race. But if politics and religion may undergo important changes, notwithstanding every opposition on the part of some superannuated politicians and divines, why should we not amend our criminal codes in spite of every resistance offered by some judicial antiquarians? Behold one, two, or three nations, which rise above a thousand others, to tell them: we embraced Christianity because this religion seemed to us more consistent than mythology; we preferred a republican government to any sort or form of monarchy, because we believed that the liberty of man is better off in the former than it can be in the latter. Well!—But if we admire those people who have spoken so, and acted in accordance with their words, why should we be astonished to see a society addressing thus its neighbours: Whereas, we have ascertained that capital punishment is neither a part of our rights nor of our wants, we reject it, we rub it off for ever from our code! Such a change, inpsired by a motive of morality, deserves more praise than a happy political revolution or religious reformation.

75. The only good reason which one may give to defend the adverse opinion, is, that political and religious changes are sometimes useful to society, whilst a murderer is for it of no profit whatever,

but, on the contrary, may prove very dangerous to its welfare. I will not deny the contingency, but I must oppose the conclusion. What should we think of a man who would say: this instrument is dangerous, and I have besides, some reason to suppose that it can be of no use, therefore I will break it, destroy it? We would, certainly, think that he reasons miserably, and acts still worse. It is not because an object, either material or rational, is dangerous, and that we know not what use to make of it, that it must be done away with; but when it is evidently demonstrated, on the one part, that it is totally useless, and on the other, that its destruction is of a positive advantage for those who own it. Now, is this the case with respect to murderers? No. I have already shown how their life can be profitable, and should be made such in favour of such citizens as have been injured by the murder. Then, it remains to prove that the execution of an assassin is of no use to society, whether we have in view the necessity of freeing it from every further fear, of putting an end to a poisonous reptile creeping into its very bosom, or impressing such as may feel disposed to turn murderers with a salutary fright. I will easily do it.

76. Here is a highway assassin! His rifle caused fright and horror to resound on all sides. His mind has interrogated crime as an honest man would interrogate benevolence. He calculated the chances, good or bad, according to his depraved judgment, of every murder which he resolved to perpetrate. Theft, arson, rape, maiming, are things very familiar to him. He has lived in the habit of spilling human blood without remorse. Often has he, without quivering, washed in roaring torrents his assassinating hands. Neither the sight of a sky torn by lightning, nor the fury of a violent storm raging on earth, have ever been able to disturb his cold undaunted villany. He laughs at virtue. Every thing in nature agrees to

accuse, to condemn, to curse him. The echoes of valleys, the shadows of night, the low, confused, painful complaints, or noisy, lacerating, thunder-like sounds of the wind in a dark thickly planted forest, the wild, boisterous, tempest-born tumult of an angry sea, the roar itself of ferocious beasts, cannot deter him from his flagitious life. The fearful cries of childhood, the powerless contempt of old age, the anxious sighs of women, the formidable oaths of manhood betray his presence wherever he goes.— Will Providence let him always tread with impunity the road of wickedness, and cause mankind to shudder before him? No. He is now arrested. All nature is hushed. The songs of victory resound joyful and loud around the car on which he lays loaded with chains. Justice holds him up to infamy and shame. Vengeance, blood-thirsty vengeance smiles at last through the iron rails of his dungeon. Innocence itself asks for his death; and every one swears that he will see him executed and throw on his corpse an everlasting impreeation.

However, justice, which likes to strike guilt with a calm, slow, solemn certainty, makes him pass from one humiliation to another. It prepares him, inch by inch, as it were, for his last expiation. The horrors of a blood-stained grave visit him the one after the other with a sanguinary display. His trial is conducted with a refined cruelty, and his condemnation seems to be for him the excruciating commencement of an unbearable eternity. Like a reprobate in hell he wanders night and day, as if pursued on every side by the threatening shadows of death, which alone reign in his dungeon and fill his mind with horror. Reduced to quail, he who was accustomed to spread terror, and fully apprized of the deep hatred which he has provoked, he dreads the scaffold less than he does public vengeance. All men appear to him like as many foes. He sees them infuriated, hastening around his executioner, snatching his doomed body from the hands of the law, and tearing it to pieces to quench their rage. But this is a mistake.

Ever since he was sentenced, the spirit of revenge with which the community were animated, has been superseded by a feeling of pity. His accusers lament now his fate. A deep silence prevails around the boards upon which the axe or the rope is waiting for him. The bloody preparations of the executioner inspire with horror all those who stand by. Curiosity is changed into torpor. Had those persons there assembled, the firm belief that they are the authors of the punishment which is to be inflicted, they would ascend the scaffold, free the culprit from death, lead him back to his dungeon, leave him there unmolested, and go home themselves with the persuasion of having performed an honorable deed. But the law orders them to retire low spirited, afflicted, scandalized. A singular portion, indeed, to bestow upon them!

77. But, perhaps, we shall discover the pretended advantage of capital punishment, in the precautionary measures which the law orders with regard to the culprit, and the morality which accompanies his sentence?—I am afraid we shall not. Behold here a man waiting in a solitary cell for the hour on which a guillotine, a wheel, a pyre, a rope, will be ready to take his life!—What his crime may be, I have not to inquire or tell for the present. The only thing which I have now to consider is, that there he lays, whatever his character may be, or is supposed to be, with an iron chain which girds his body and entangles his legs and arms; every possible means of escape is taken from him; he can hardly use his feet and hands without experiencing some pain in his bones, muscles, and nerves. Chained at an equal distance from an iron trap, the image for him of a tomb stone, and from a window, through the rails of which comes, to tantalize him, the sweet breeze of a fresh, seducing atmosphere, he can neither touch the one to try its strength, nor walk to the other to breathe

a better air. A turnkey is commissioned to watch over him day and night, to preserve him for the executioner. As for his judge, he is gone home to converse with his family and friends, and take a good, hearty dinner, after having left to the sad echoes of the cell in which he sent the culprit, these curious if not truly mocking words: "Man! thou art convicted and condemned: prepare for death! thou hast no other help or support left but that from above, and no other hope to rely upon except that of thy faith in the life to come. Cursed as thou art by thy fellow-beings in the name of the law, thou canst only converse with thy God, until I will send thee to him for ever. He may be a father to thee, but we are no more thy brothers, though we say he is our father; he may grant thee life, but we will kill thee; if heaven is for thee, so much the better; but earth reproves thee, I cannot help it; the mercies of Jesus will, most likely, or rather if thou choosest, be a compensation for our revengeful feelings; but we must have rerevenge; so, supplicate the mercy of thy good Maker, for we, men, judge proper to behead, to hang, to burn thee! Set the affairs of thy conscience for the better, so that when we do away with thy body, thy soul may receive its share of the heavenly blessings, breathe the holy perfumes of the eternal Eden, inhale the pure joys of angels, and wear peacefully the evergreen laurels of a glorious immortality! But in as much as I am concerned, I curse thee again. Farewell!"

78. I will make no commentaries upon such a proceeding; facts speak loudly enough by themselves. But I will ask: Who can believe that a man thus immured and harangued, will resign himself to his fate, and obey the impertinent sermon of a laypreacher? Nobody. Why? Because if that man obeyed, Capital punishment, far from being an advantage for society, would be nothing more or less than a stupid act of barbarity. I will explain this conclusion. So far as we admit that there is no vice that

cannot be corrected, no rogue that cannot turn an honest man if he chooses, and be as useful to society as he was dangerous to it; it is evident that when a man repents of his crime, abhors its consequences, makes ready to repair the wrongs which he has done, yields sincerely to religion, and to virtue, we should not kill him. A punishment which tends to mock repentance is a cruelty that has no name but in hell; and it is scandalous, anti-Christian, anti-social, that men, civilized by the religion of Christ, should be more severe than he is, and dare to strike to death those of his followers whom his divine hand will spare!

79. Methinks it would be more rational, and also more in accordance with the principles of our gospel, that societies which believe in it, and consider as the best inspirer of every social compact its divine hero, would consent to acknowledge the rights which a converted rogue has to the mercy of his fellow-worshippers. Were it so, men would be on earth what Christ is in heaven; like him, they would hope and wait for the conversion of villains, and rejoice more at the return of a lost one into the social pale than they do at the persevering honesty of ninety-nine other citizens. But there is an antipathy to mercy in this world. The same men who follow obstinately a few extraordinary examples of revenge, mentioned in the Jewish testament, refuse to be animated with the spirit of pardon which breathes in every page of the Christian gospel. They force into their codes a sanguinary theocracy, and they resist the inspirations of a divine philanthropy, and decide that it is better to kill than to correct. Then, to what purpose the sermon of a judge! To what advantage the punishment!

80. A vain philosophy is not to be invoked here in favour of society! The more we will investigate its conduct with regard to the present question, the more we will find that its laws and practice contradict each other; that both are contrary to reason and good faith. On the one side, it decides that the

convict should repent, acknowledge his depravity and confess his crime for the repose of his judge's conscience; receive and welcome priests; finish well, with their help, a life badly spent: and, on the other, it acts with him as if he was necessarily a hypocrite, refuses to forgive him on the ground that, if amendment was a sufficient motive of pardon, no bandit could be found who would not wrap himself, at least apparently, with the cloak of repentance. But, let us suppose that such may, in some instances, be the case: what of it? Nothing, except that it shows how limited human intellect is; how little acquainted we are with the inward passions of man. What remains after such an excuse, alleged by a villain? Nothing, but a doubt. Then, if our criminal courts, placed as they are between society, which trusts them with its interests and safety, and a convict who protests in favour of his regrets and repentance, choose to sacrifice the latter, it is evident that they act less through conviction than through complacency—that which is very wrong. Is there no means by which they would be able to satisfy both their responsibility as judges, and their consciences as men? Yes, there is one. Of the two evils left to their disposal, viz: a prison or death, let them choose, the least in itself, and, most probably, the most efficacious in its results; that is to say, a prison. If the culprit repents, confinement should please him; and he will, no doubt, accept it with its troubles and long duration, because he will understand its comparative necessity in a situation like his. And supposing that he is but a hypocrite, his punishment will be severer, inasmuch as despair and grief, which remain, will torment him more, and may, possibly, incline him to repentance. Experience has proved it; the gloomy silence of a dungeon speaks powerfully of heaven, and intimates sorrow, whilst the scandalous bustle of a scaffold prepares guilt to meet fearlessly with the horrors of hell.

81. All those philanthropists who have visited

such convicts as are sentenced to death, and who have, also, taken some trouble in investigating the second nature of those wretches, know well that repentance operates less than hatred and vengeance upon them. By dint of cursing continually their accusers and judges, they fall actually into an error with regard to their real position, finish by forgetting altogether that they are guilty of the crime for which they are condemned to die, and invoke, most seriously, the justice of God against all those whom they consider, in earnest, as their foes. They entertain the clergymen who call at the jail to assist them, not with their sins and crimes, as one might suppose, but with their unmerited sufferings and unaccountable misfortune; the effects, and not the shame of a scaffold, affect them, torture them. They complain of being abandoned by heaven, and will utter against it the most horrid blasphemies. Their pale, anxious, hypocritical faces deceive often both priests and jailers: one would think that they are exhausted, almost dead, whilst they are preparing secretly their strength, their courage of mind for the day of their execution, when they will appear proud as a hero, calm as a poor, wrongly condemned innocent. I understand that. They have henceforth nothing to lose or fear; their reputation is spotted over with stains of blood; the imprecations of men are familiar to them. You believe that your presence saddens them, that they listen to your good counsels, and will avail themselves of your philanthropy! but you are mistaken. They see nothing but the walls of the dungeon, in which every hope is taken from them; they obey exclusively one single, favourite idea, that of escaping justice. That idea, natural enemy of every amendment, keeps their mind attentive and uneasy; they stare all the time at the grim gate, which never moves on its hinges but to terrify them, and let all sorts of heart-rending furies enter with Despair in their last abode. As long as they thought of avoiding death, they lived upon dissimulation, tried to inspire their jailers with a feeling of compassion, and to persuade the visiters that they were innocent; but as soon as the fatal hour comes, they curse human justice, they would kill its officers if they could, and if all the legal supports of judicial murder were not standing around to protect the execution of the law, to secure their necks for the knife or the rope, they could, in a paroxysm of anger, cut their way to freedom through a stream of blood. They pass suddenly from calmness to despair, from despair to calmness; they do, at the same time, cry and laugh, sigh and swear, raise with an indomitable pride their doomed heads, and let them fall with an inconsolable grief on their labouring breasts. They call for a priest, they pray, they seem sorry, repentant, converted; but crime heaves still in their hearts, and death finds it yet in their throats, if I can say so, when it stifles their last breath on the scaffold. Hence those scandalous confessions which many of them leave on their coffins in Protestant countries! Those sorrowless avowals with which they afflict Catholic clergymen in some other places! Let us say it with a profitable terror! If our Christian religion is true, and I think it is, out of a hundred men killed in the name of the law on scaffolds, ninety-five, at least, pass from the hands of their executioners into the grasp of Satan. Two examples, among a thousand others, will give an idea of such a frightful fall.

82. "Not long ago, a young priest, newly ordained, and animated with that sincere and heart-felt persuasion which qualifies every where the pious guests of our ecclesiastical seminaries, was called to assist at the last moments of a murderer. He was chained to a thick wall, in a subterraneous dungeon, bending under the weight of his irons, squatted, as it were, on a bunch of straw, which he had ground with his gnashing teeth, piece by piece, to make it softer, looked from afar like a tiger watching for the passage of its prey, moved like a horrid snake which is,

at the same time, excited and terrified by a hydra with a hundred heads.—Neither the chaplain of the jail, nor the sisters of charity had been able to touch his heart. He swore and blasphemed like a demon, mocked both religion and the law with an equal contempt, compared, sneeringly, God with the jury who had condemned him, and confounded them together, in the incessant curses which his poisoned tongue threw up to the echoes of the vault, built, by social fear, over the head of crime.

"No one, I say, had dared, ever since justice struck him, to approach nearer than the door of his dungeon. So, the presence of a priest yet young and almost a child, as he said, seemed to astonish his pride, when he saw him standing calm and resigned by his side. He contemplated him without uttering a single word, or allowing his breast to heave with a single sigh, so expressive of goodness and virtue was the modest and simple look of the missionary. Such was his surprise and silence that one would have said that, forgetful of his own passions, he enjoyed the anxiety and pity which the sight of a reprobate like him appeared to have inspired a man of God. It was a sort of a transient triumph of hell over heaven, a living exemplification of that contemptuous smile with which the prince of darkness looks at the cross of Jesus, an hypocritical peace, the forerunner of a deadly war.—At last, the veil of falsehood fell from his face. He rose like a monster in a human frame; his chains rattled on his emaciated legs; he moved a few paces forwards, burst into a tumultuous laughter, and let his teeth chatter horribly. A deep, long suppressed, ferocious groan started from his shattered heart, and his flagitious thoughts flew out from his crime frothing mouth with this desolating eloquence: 'Imprudent young man, what do you want here? Who sends you to me? You think, perhaps, that the stamp of ignominy which justice has impressed on my forehead, authorizes you to come and disturb, with impunity, my silent rest in this dungeon!—It has been lent to me for a few weeks, during which, I dare to say, no one can pass its threshold without my consent.—Men may chain my body which they have caught by dint of cunning, like the hunter his prey; I do not dispute their power so far; but my thoughts, sir, my thoughts are yet my own property, for I have made them by myself.—Yes! I am their author, their king, their only master. They are mine, I say, and I do pretend that no man whosoever should presume to control them, in any way, to bring them to any account, unless I allow him to visit and question me. Your youth is a legitimate excuse for your temerity.—I will admit it. But let me tell you that, in spite of all your virtue, you have as yet no experience. At your age and in your situation, a man knows nothing of life except what is good and admirable in it. You think that it depends upon man to do so and so, at his option, that evil should be made good, as good is made evil. That is a mistake, young man, and a great one too!—instructed in a better school, I think, Priest! I know more than you can can possibly know, at least about the defects of our nature!—Then listen to me!—What I was bound to do I have done. I can neither accuse myself nor repent of my deeds. I have contemplated the scaffold from the very day on which I decided to brave it. How can I be astonished, now that I see it raised for me, asking coldly for my blood and life?—Both belong to it. It may take both at any time it pleases. I decline not to pay my debts.—As I had nothing in this world, I wished to become rich. I thought of acquiring wealth. I began to apply myself at an honest trade as men say. That trade proved to be of no use to me. I embraced another, it was worse. Meanwhile I was hungry, thirsty, without clothing and lodging. I asked for assistance as a man should ask, politely, gentlemanly. I was refused. Then I went to implore pity like a beggar. I was despised. The one said I was an idle fellow; the other remembered having seen me enter drinking places; a few gave me some cents; but all the rest trampled upon me. I could bear it no longer. I armed against a society which treated me so badly. I went into a forest, and from there on the highway. You may believe that at first, fear, remorse, religion, and all those means of an egotistical morality which old and rich people teach to children and to the poor, preyed upon me, and kept me, as you who are a clergyman would say, in the path of virtue. But these prejudices soon vanished before the want which urged me. Since I cannot have any thing unless I steal it, I will steal; and if, to steal with impunity, I have to kill, I will kill!—So did I speak within myself during a stormy night which I spent poor, destitute, hungry, on a highway. One lost traveller having, at last, passed by me, I stopped him. He resisted. I killed him.—Ever since I never felt embarrassed in the least, when I had to spill blood; and I do not yet see why I should have hesitated!—Notwithstanding what one may say about my profession, I never was able to distinguish it from the life of a duellist who kills for his pleasure, from the wanderer of the mountain so celebrated in Asia, and whose occupation it was to assassinate, from the famous Napoleon the bastard son of the French revolution.—Like the duellist and the wanderer, this conqueror fought every body, attacked every body.—Well! I have done nothing but imitate him.—however, we finish quite differently.—Blood brought him power; and it drags me to a scaffold. He died glorious. I will perish cursed by every body. So goes the world. I do not complain. I should know what I was preparing just as well as he did. Each of us had been served according to his expectations. I will ascend the scaffold as he ascended his throne, satisfied with my deeds and rewards as much as he was with his.—And what does it matter to me, if men, who praise him, blame me!—I am a bandit, will they say!—Yes, I am. Nay, I have the conscience of a brigand; but,

Priest! you may believe me, such a conscience is worth that of a conqueror and perhaps more.—That is all I have to say. Please to let me alone, unless you think that my company is as good as another for you.—If so, you may remain. You please me. I have no objection to be your friend!'

"My friend!" exclaimed the priest, whom the wicked philosophy of the convict had affected deeply. "My friend! oh, yes, and what is by far better, my brother! You weak, unfortunate, almost lost man! In the name of God, I beg you will listen to me as calmly as I listened to you. I come not to hurt your feelings, to quarrel with you, and to fill your last days with an useless bitterness; but I come with charitable thoughts in my mind, merciful sensations in my heart, soothing words on my lips. Listen to me! With men like you, reproaches, sermons, mystic remarks would, perhaps, be of no use. I see, you have weighed, measured, divided crime in your hours of leisure. Indeed, you were wrong to do so; but, however dangerous that practice was, however fatal it proves to be now with regard to you, it may still turn to be profitable if you will change its object. Try to study, to understand, to embrace virtue as you have done its adversary. Why would you not? The mind which was able to conceive and execute evil so well as yours did, can also appreciate good duly, and practise it with some advantage. Confess it with sincerity. This fatal idea of yours, that we are either religious or virtuous but in consequence of a long imbibed prejudice, has gradually led you into incredulity, from incredulity to despair, from despair to crime, from crime to the miserable condition which is now your last in this world. You despise men because some of them ill-treated you. You mistrust priests because they speak to you of virtue. You will not pray because you think that all that we do is the result of a blind, unimpeachable necessity. You believe that our Christian faith is no remedy for your soul, because this faith can no more, it seems, answer the numberless wants of a guilty conscience. But you are mistaken. It is habit and not conviction, which causes you to reject both the counsels and consolations of true piety. Listen to me again! Your language, your thoughts, your wild eloquence, betray your good, honest origin. These rags, symbols of deep and irretrievable misery, which now cover your body, assimilate you with wretched men and seem to veil your real character. But your ideas of things, whilst they come out grand and sublime, though criminal, adorned with the dazzling gems of science, though tinged with the spurious colours of depravity, tell me clearly that you have seen noble, pure, happy days. No! you were not born to stoop so low, to die so soon; and yet, here you are on the brink of a horrible abyss into which you are doomed to fall. Your days are numbered; they will soon pass by. A few more of them, and the rays of the sun which shines over your head, shall shine only upon your grave. Then, before you descend into it, call back the pure thoughts and harmless feelings of your boyhood. Enter into your heart again, examine it, open it to me, that I may console you, enlighten you, save you. Oh, how glad I will be if you judge me worthy of your confidence! Confidence, my dear sir, is the first step we take towards friendship, and friendship, pure friendship, remember it, leads us to heaven."

"Enough! young man, enough!" replied, suddenly, the convict: "you speak like an angel, like a God: your mild, charitable, rational speech has soothed my anger. Your unexpected but welcome visit has made me feel once more happy. You are more than a priest; you are a man acquainted with the miseries of this vale of perdition and lust. I am sorry I was, at first, so rude to you. Here is my hand! take it, press it friendly within yours! I wish that all those who were allowed to press it before had trembled as you do, perhaps, you would not have now the trouble of pitying my unhappy fate. I was, indeed, far, very far, this morning, from supposing that I would welcome so friendly the sensations long past and almost forgotten of my youth. Well! let them come back to my memory, and be perused by it! It is comfortable to recall, before death, associations which I thought had departed for ever. I feel I have some tears left to honour this unexpected visit. Behold! my dear sir! they rise in my sad eyes, they flow slowly but sweetly on my burning cheeks, they drop on my bloody hands as cold as ice but as refreshing as love. Good heavens! how I delight in shedding them! how pleasant, how alleviating it is to cry and sob! Pray, young man, let me alone with my recollections; let me alone with my father and mother, with my schoolmates, with my last pleasure, that of regret! Your presence here renders me uneasy now. I look at you and my thoughts vanish, my thoughts which I want to resume, which I am delighted to feel, as they were, when I used to play on the lap of my poor, afflicted, dishonoured mother! Ah! pray, leave me! I wish, I demand to be left alone!"

"A torrent of tears accompanied these words. He fell back on his straw, sobbed deeply, and seemed to yield himself to the impressions of virtue. The priest believed that he was touched, converted, preparing to be reconciled with God, and that, on the next day, the divine grace would restore to heaven an unfortunate wretch whom the foe of our race had led astray. Alas! he was deceived. Nature, but not religion, had spoken in the heart of the convict. An abyss of crime, as he had never seen before except in the awful description of our holy writers, was now to open vast, bottomless, horrible, blood-tinged before the priest.

"On the next morning, as he entered the dungeon to tell the convict that every hope of pardon was gone, and that a scaffold was waiting for its victim, a terrific, ghastly shriek answered his sighs and pious entreaties. Wickedness had been stronger than grace, and the pride of crime had overpowered the prayers of virtue. 'Well sir,' cried the convict, 'if it is so, let death and its ministers come in! I am ready. As for you, just, good, honest man, whom I revere, though I have no belief in your theology, stand aside! You will be able to see how those men whom society pretends to curse, know how to brave shame, infamy, death! Look at me patiently, as long as they are preparing my body for their sanguinary purpose! then, when they take me out, follow my steps with courage, and quit me not, but when life is extinct, and when this tongue which now addresses you so deliberately has become speechless; you will see whether I shake, whether I keep perfectly composed, from the time I leave this damp couch up to that in which they will tie me upon the fatal boards. Ah! I defy them all! I laugh at them all! I am as grand as they are strong! feel my pulse, if you doubt what I say, reverend sir! the regularity of its motions will testify better than my words, the calmness of my soul, supposing that I have one. You believe that I have, and I do not. That is the only difference which exists between your philosophy and mine, but it is a material one: therefore cease to try the effects of your pious reasonings, charitable views, and Christian hopes upon me! it would be useless, my mind is made up with respect to all that, I believe it not; but that which I must have a full faith in is, that my last hour has struck!'—and, turning to the executioners, he added, 'walk in, therefore, ye butchers! walk in! here lies my body! take it, cut it and mangle it as you please!'

"The chief executioner entered; the jailer, as the law directs, delivered to him the convict; and every thing being ready, all went out together between a dense row of police officers. The priest, of course, was following, but endeavoured vainly to approach, to exhort, to convert the criminal; horrible blasphemies answered his supplications, and his pious admonitions were laughed at. That villain, being once seated on the stone bench of the prison yard, where it was customary to take off the iron collar and chain from those cadaverous preys of judicial severity, smiled with scorn on the vestment of death with which they wrapped him up, tried with his freed hands the strength of his doomed neck, asked for a bottle of wine, which he quaffed gaily, lighted a segar, began smoking, and appeared boldly before the people, who waited anxiously for him in the street. The sight of an immense, numberless, curious, impatient crowd produced no change on his features, he appeared always the same; his step was firm, his head erect, his look bold; and when he saw himself tied to the guillotine, he measured impudently the height of the scaffold, bowed to the spectators, sent to them a last puff of smoke, smiled on the priest, in bidding him farewell, and fell into the dreadful mysteries of eternity without repenting for what he had done.—Is it not a horrible death?—And, let no person say that such a depravity is rare! It is not with great criminals and highway murderers of whom I now speak. Most part of them die in the same manner.—Then where is the neccessity, the profitable necessity of presenting society with scenes so bloody?"

83. The next example tends to acquaint the reader with the effects of hypocrisy in a villain's heart. I have received it from the same clergyman, who related to me this disgraceful history, as follows:

"A brigand had been found guilty of twelve rapes, of arson in six different places, and of five murders on the highway. Sentence of death was, according to the verdict, brought in, and passed upon him: they threw his body in a dungeon, sixty feet under ground; a lofty, sombre, heavy tower stood over him. As soon as he was shut up and chained there, he began to utter lamentations, which, for forty consecutive hours, resounded along the vaults and gloomy staircases of his prison; but, exhausted at last, and reduced to silence, he fell on his irons and slept in the arms of despair. The jailer thought that he would begin anew to make the echoes of the place resound with his oaths and screams, when awakened. Not at all; a sudden change had been operated in him; he was quiet, and looked dejected. They questioned him about his health. He said he was well, protested his innocence with an air of profound humility, refused to take any food, and called calmly for death, which he besought fervently to visit him before the executioner came to break his chains and claim his body. Such was his apparent dejection, that the turnkeys themselves pitied him. Every time they opened his cell, he asked for the sisters of charity, at whose feet he knelt, crying for mercy; desired to have by him a priest, whose hands he kissed as a poor penitent,—whose blessings he begged as a persecuted innocent; and when the jailer came in, he would shed abundant tears, supplicate for an alleviation of his sufferings, swear that he would wait patiently for his unhappy end, provided they consented to shut him up in a less horrid place; in a word, he played so well the new character which he had assumed, that he deceived every body, priests, judges and jailers.

"They took him out of the dungeon, and gave him a strong-built cell in the prison-yard. There he could see the sun, and talk with the prisoners from the window, or wicket. He seemed also to be contented, resigned, happy, as much as one can be who is condemned to an ignominious death. The visits of a sister of charity, commissioned to attend to him, pleased him, and calmed his grief. At least so they thought. He used, likewise, to welcome the priest with that sensitive eagerness which persecuted virtue does commonly show for the succours and consolations of piety. Nay, his daily, expressed wish was that they would allow him to go to confession, hear mass, and receive the sacrament in the chapel. He spoke of heaven like an elect, prayed for his accusers, blessed his judges, and would have kissed the very hands of his executioner, had he been present. The cross of Jesus was the usual subject of his conversation, which tended always to establish his innocence. Who would have thought that a man so fond of praying, so ready to pardon, was, indeed, a villain, an incendiary, a murderer?—He spoke also very frequently of an only daughter,—praised her excellent qualities and modest piety, boasted of the care he bestowed on her education:—who would have thought that such a father was but a bandit, as lascivious as he was inhuman?—Such he was, however!

"The priest, deceived, as I have said, by his hypocrisy, entertained suspicions of his guilt, regretted that the law prohibited a man sentenced to death the sacrament of the church; and thought seriously of the means he could contrive to mitigate the orders of the court, for the purpose of contenting his penitent. But God, whose providence shields the just, opposed his design!

"When he came on the following day to comply with his sad commission, and announce the coming hour of death to the convict, he was informed that he had eaten a hearty breakfast, and waited for him in the chapel's cell.

"This cell had an aperture opposite to the altar. But strong and narrowly separated iron rails secured fast in the pavement and vault of the chapel, which permitted the culprit and priest to see each other, protected perfectly the latter from every attack on the part of the former.

"As soon as he saw the priest enter the church, he knelt devoutly, and appeared to be deeply affected by this last demonstration of mistrust and severity on the side of the jailers. He said he wished to go and kneel before the altar, to serve mass and receive the sacrament, in order that he might depart for a better world, strengthened by the drink and bread of heavenly mercy; and besought his confessor to obtain this favour for him. His prayer was listened to, and the favour asked earnestly by the priest, but positively refused by the jailer.

Then, that hypocrite burst into blasphemies. He passed suddenly from his apparent repose to a diabolical excess of anger, swore horribly, intermixing with the most dreadful oaths the emphatic narration of that part of his life which had been honourable. It was a shocking sight. He would knock his head against the walls, roll himself on the pavement, curse all those whom he had blessed heretofore, insult shamelessly the holy man who endeavoured to console him, set at defiance heaven and earth, swallow pinch after pinch a poisonous dust which he had made of copper cents long dipped in a certain liquid, cut the veins of his neck with a knife he had borrowed from another convict, and threaten his confessor with these infernal exclamations; Cursed priest! thank thy God whom I despise, and my jailers whom I hate! This knife has been sharpened by me for the purpose of cutting thy throat. It was my intention to kill thee on the very altar of thy Jesus, who is not a bit better than thou art, and whom I laugh at. Thou surpassest me in falsehood and dissimulation. It was thou who didst order justice to raise this iron gate between my rage and thy lying face. Thou robbest me of my chief glory, the glory of spilling thy blood. I shall commit, then, no other murder before I die; enjoy thy cunning, cursed priest! But behold my own blood! It flows out of my own wounds. It will have done flowing before the hour of my execution strikes. They will have but a corpse to throw on their scaffold!

The priest, frightened, called for help. The jailer, armed with his sabre and pistols, rushes in the cell; police officers follow him. They snatch the knife from the convict's hands. The executioner seizes him, cuts quickly his hair, ties his hands, tears his shirt, throws him on a car, and leads him slowly amidst a crowd assembled to witness this bloody scene to the place of execution.

"Every one thought him already dead, for he appeared motionless between the executioner and the priest. But it was another of his damnable plots. In a moment when the attention of these seemed diverted towards other objects, he raises as if to utter a painful sigh, shakes his shoulders, aims at the priest whom he knocks on the breast with his head, and bursts into a terrible laughter, as he sees the man of God grow pale, stagger, fall breathless under the wheels of the car. The people infuriated, rush tumultuously between the car and the scaffold. They want to drag him down, and tear him to pieces; but the law intervenes, the executioner grasps his prey again, and the priest, always calm, unshaken, zealous for the soul of the villain, pacifies the mob with a word of forbearance, ascends his place a second time, and prays again to God for the conversion of his foe. The car proceeds, arrives, stops finally at the foot of the fatal boards.

"But there, a new scandal takes place. The executioner is obliged to place his resisting prey on his shoulders, and to carry him up on the scaffold where he stands at last exposed to the gaze of the people, whilst they tie him to the guillotine. The spectators look at him, and feel moved with horror at the sight of the dark, clotted blood, which runs around the neck of the wretch. Poison is impregnated in the disgusting foam which flows from his dying mouth; his bewildered eye seeks for the image of Jesus; the priest presents it to him; he sees it, insults it, spits on it at the very moment in which the fatal machinery hurls him before the tribunal of God; and, thus refusing the divine aid of mercy, he falls into the scourging arms of a pitiless justice. I ask it again: What is the use to afflict the eyes of men with such horrors?"

84. We have just seen two men, the first of whom had embraced and followed the career of a murderer, as a general would that of a conqueror; and the second had abandoned himself to wickedness through a passion for blood, veiled with the appear-

ances of virtue. Of what use was the scaffold to them? The latter had hoped that he would render his punishment conspicuous by a crime as yet unheard-of—I mean, the murder of his father-confessor; and the former considered this public atonement of his life as the glorious term of the sanguinary fame which he had obtained. It was, on the one side, a long-meditated and boasted avowal of a life spent without any principle of equity, and made an enemy of remorse; and, on the other, a hypocritical denegation of crime, based upon a horrible desire of illustrating his exit by an act still more atrocious. Such beings, I dare to say, would have been punished more efficaciously if a perpetual silence in a solitary dungeon had answered their insulting and bloody ambition. The very thought that the remembrance of their crimes would gradually perish with all but themselves, and that they were to live only in shame and despair before God, whilst they would be forgotten on earth, should have sooner or later prevailed; and, perhaps, regret, which often springs from the contempt of mankind, would have operated more efficaciously than a punishment legally inflicted. When infamy ceases to be a motive of pride, it turns, commonly, into an occasion of repentance!

85. There are also convicts, to whom it is of importance, whether for themselves or for their families, not to confess the crime which leads them to death. Accordingly, they deny to the last, and die unrepentant. Others, on the contrary, look at their deeds of blood with an eye of complacency,—boast of them, tell their motives, details and results, less to humiliate themselves than to entertain the public, and avoid, through the interest which they endeavour to inspire, the malediction which they deserve. Some, like the two whose end I have described, mock God and hate men; for them, no doubt, capital punishment is a mere consequence which they wish to make coincide with its principle, and thus deceive

the hopes of human justice. There are a few, however, who tremble and repent on reviewing their monstrous conduct. All the objects around them look to them as if they were tinged with blood. They accept, with an exemplary resignation, grief, infamy and death, which is a real benefit for them. Their execution afflicts more than it instructs; the people are sorry to see, in the hands of a hangman, beings whom a momentary error made criminal; whom shame purifies, and the scaffold helps to heaven. I will bring here an example, which I have from the same authority, and which will tend to confirm this last observation.

86. "A merchant who had suddenly become rich, had a daughter as handsome, and as amiable, as well educated; he had spared neither time nor money to render her worthy of a world to which she belonged not, but to which she was to have an access through an uncle, on her mother's side, which uncle, thanks to his well known merits, filled one of the highest offices in his country. Unhappily, fortune, which laughs at our pride and mocks our hopes, abandoned that merchant. From the rich and influential citizen he had been, he became poor and unnoticed. Perhaps he would have consented to be forgotten, ill-treated by men, if he had been alone on earth, for poverty is nothing in itself; but he thought of his daughter and wept bitterly. 'Is it true then,' said he, 'that a clown shall marry her! that poor child for whose sake I have toiled so much, who is only accustomed to what is sweet, agreeable, and full of the illusions of youth, shall henceforth endure all that is sour, hard, and really rigorous in it? Oh! that is too much for my mind to think, and for my heart to bear. I will die! . . . . . : But if I die, will she suffer less? On the contrary, the recollection of my sorrows will press on her whose happiness was the aim of all my efforts. Oh! how often did she appear to me full of grace and glorious hopes, like the evening star of my life! How often have I seen her

rich, beautiful, and happy, in my dreams! Now, I am doomed to live only to be made sensible that she is more afflicted, sadder, poorer than any other girl. Unhappy daughter! unhappy father!'

"Alas! he spoke truly: but how far was he in the mean time from suspecting in what manner his prophecy would be accomplished! As he went, exhausted by the labour of his mind, which was filled with regrets for the past, horror for the present, and fear for the future, he met, by chance in his way, one of those men whom the god of wealth is pleased to favour so much the more as the goddess of beauty seems to have despised and abandoned them: I mean a very rich but very ugly nobleman. This one, seduced by the charms of the girl, asks for her hand; the father, informed that his child disliked such a lover, hesitates, refuses him at first, but he remonstrates at home, begs her to reflect about his present situation, expresses the wish to see her make for him a painful sacrifice. That was sufficient to decide her, she accepts, she is sold, bargained for, married to supply, at the same time, the pleasure of the buyer, and alleviate the misery of the seller, who, satisfied that he had, by so doing, repaired all his wrongs towards his daughter, died soon after of old age, and left her with her wealthy husband.

"Wealthy, indeed, but also very jealous; the beauty of his wife was the cause both of his grief and his joy; every gentleman who approached her was an object of suspicion to his mind, an occasion of torture to his heart; as constant as passionate in his love, he was always upon his guard, lest his precious treasure should be stolen from him, lest another man should seduce his dear, adored half. Overpowered at last by these incessant perplexities, he left the Parisian world, took her with him, and went a hundred leagues in a province to reside with her in a solitary castle which he had inherited from his ancestors. There he met no more with such gentlemen as would inspire him with fear, and he was permitted to enjoy his happiness; nay, almost certain of a virtue which he had thus imprisoned, he dared to believe that she was content, and would love him better. But he was greatly mistaken in that supposition; his precaution caused his ruin! His unfortunate wife became irritated, and, as it is usual with women in such a case, renounced the pains of grief to enjoy the pleasures of revenge. Contempt superseded respect in her mind, hatred raged in her heart; she resolved to be untrue to her husband, and, being unable to find a man of the world with whom she would have chosen to sin, she looked, in a paroxysm of despair, for a lover among the peasants who had to obey her orders. The genius of evil, always ready to answer the mischievous calls and wishes of our kind, satisfied her depraved appetite. It brought her into the company of a young miller, whose noble countenance and genteel figure seduced her. Pleased with him, but still fearful, she addressed him, at first, as it becomes a fashionable lady. He did not understand. Accustomed to bend before a master, the poor fellow yielded to a feeling of affection for his lord's lady, and the more she provoked him, the more she commanded a respect which she desired to change into the freedom of dishonourable love. Nothing was obtained until she ordered him to come to her room. There he was to perish. Surprised, moved, seduced, as it were, at the sight of an elegant, richly furnished, luxurious boudoir, he felt love enter his heart; he blushed, sighed, declared his passion, and found it reciprocal; both fell in a common abyss of crime and misery, and would to God they had been satisfied with that inexcusable violation of the most sacred rights! But vice never stops when it has once begun its dreadful career. The miller, unfit for a favour which he would not have dared even to think of, abused it; and became soon the tyrant of a heart which loved him to distraction. Amidst the intoxicating conversations which their lust occasioned, he undertook to criticise bitterly his master, and wish for his death; a reprehensible want of liberty caused the lady to listen to him; she reciprocated his desires: they talked of an elopement, then of a crime; and the tongue of unchaste desire utters the thoughts of a vile murderer! One day, their passion having spoken with more violence than usual, they swore they would get rid of a man who rose every morning to oppose their unlawful happiness, and, as prompt as the fire which devoured them both, they accomplished their fatal oath during the night which followed. Confiding, as I have said, in the virtue of his wife, and believing himself far from every danger, her husband had retired early, and was fast asleep. They choked him in his bed, whilst a deep silence prevailed in the house; he died without uttering a single cry that might have betrayed either his sufferings or his murderers. The next day, it was reported that the gentleman had a violent attack of apoplexy, which carried him off suddenly. Every one believed that it was true; the priest of the parish was called for, he buried the corpse, a few regrets accompanied this sad ceremony, oblivion came soon after, and crime seemed to have triumphed with impunity over a grave. But Providence would not permit the guilty to escape long; their own imprudence betrayed them; the lady testified too little grief, and the miller began to enjoy sooner than he should the fruits of his bloody deed. On seeing him enter the mansion of his dead master, as if he had been his successor, some persons suspected that all was not right; they expressed their suspicions loudly, justice was informed, its officers appeared, the corpse was taken out of its coffin and examined carefully, evident marks of strangulation were discovered around the neck, the murder was ascertained beyond a doubt, and upon the accusation of some neighbours, the guilty pair were arrested, tried, convicted, and sentenced to death.

"Behold, then, a lady who was born happy and rich, now doomed to misery! Though connected with a grandee of the State to which she belonged, and an associate of the fashionable world, she lays in a dungeon, and waits for an ignominious death! Now, shall such a death be inflicted upon her? All that credit and money can do among men will be tried. The court of appeals is petitioned that it may, at least, find a motive to annul the judgment. Vain effort! Skill, bribery, prayers, all is useless. The sentence is confirmed. She shall be executed, unless the king who has the power to pardon, will take into consideration the circumstances of the crime, and favour the afflicted family of the criminal; but, alas! the king refuses to listen, the king says: "Let justice be done!

"The lady, however, had become a lamentable prey to her remorse, and shed, every day, abundant tears. Less frightened by the sight of a scaffold than tormented by the stings of her conscience, she repented, and paid a due justice to the man whom she had sacrificed to her hatred at a time in which it was yet in her power to choose between resignation and dishonour. She understood, though too late, that his love was fond and passionate, that he would have been neither so severe nor so jealous, had he not been so ugly: that the bitter reproaches which he made her during his life should have been a proof of his tender feelings rather than a motive for her bloody deed, and that, by murdering him, she had immolated to her unruled passions not only a husband worthy of respect, but also a true, sincere lover. So death seemed to her a just punishment; nay, she desired to suffer it, because she hoped that, through it, she might expiate her crime before men and save her soul from perdition. 'What can I do, now, on earth, said she to her confessor, if the king pardons me? I thank you, my father, for the consolation which you bring me, and for the hope which you would make me entertain, but I neither can cherish the one, nor accept the other; though you say, my conscience tells me that there is no rest for crime, no retrieval from the abyss into which I have willingly fallen. Life would be for me but a heavy, unbearable burden. The blood stained ghost of my murdered husband disturbs my sleep. I dream of him every night. His image pursues me during the day: methinks, I see it on whatever side I allow my eyes to wander in this narrow, dreary dungeon. The least noise I hear, the very rustling of these rags, miserable remnants of a once rich attire, the crackling of this straw which bends or breaks under my exhausted frame, the water which falls from this damp vault upon the flags below, drop by drop, like the slow, heart-rending sounds of a death-tolling clock, every thing frightens me, and renders life insupportable. Indeed, my father, I will be glad when they come to behead me! The efforts of my family tend only to protract my torments. I have deserved to finish on a scaffold my guilty life. The hand of an executioner will be less cruel than the pity of a king. And what have I to dread now?—shame? alas! I see it continually rising like a threatening phantom before me. It surrounds me like a vestment of malediction. It pervades all my senses, it torments, it chokes me mercilessly. The contempt and hateful look of that multitude which will assemble to see me die!—but, my father, is that contemptuous and hateful look to be compared to the inward scorn which my conscience and my restless imagination force me to endure when they tell me incessantly that I am a vile murderer, and thus torture me almost to madness. Sufferings!—oh! heavens! should there be men who believe that the sharp blade of a heavy, triangular hanger is more to be dreaded than an endless remorse; that a head severed by a single stroke of a knife, undergoes a more grievous punishment than a head filled with terrors, besieged by a thousand devouring, excruciating thoughts! Ah! if they believe it, they are labouring under the grossest error, my father! They know not what sufferings are! Life, should justice condemn me now to pass it in a lonesome cell, amidst the horrors of remorse, life would be a more severe punishment than death. I feel it. No, no! let me die! My death is necessary. Blood must atone for blood. Let them spill mine to-morrow, yes, to-morrow. The execution of a vile but repentant woman will be a public reparation for her wickedness; and when I die an object of horror and scorn before the world, perhaps my humiliation will be serviceable to me at the awful bar of a God as merciful as he is just, of a God whose pardon I implore, kneeling and confessing my crime before you, my good father.' So did she speak whenever the priest entered her dungeon! It was evident that a sincere horror of her deed raged in her mind, that sincere feelings of repentance filled her broken heart. God was satisfied; but it remained that men were so, that their curiosity knew those afflicting secrets which religion alone had contemplated in her prison.

"The presence of an executioner did not astonish her. She welcomed him, and gave herself up to him with an edifying resignation. The sudden passage of his scissors around her neck, grown snow white by the effects of fear and grief, at first caused her to shake slightly, and seeing her beautiful hair fall at her feet, she shed a solitary tear, and sobbed deeply; but raising her eyes to heaven, she whispered a prayer, and then stood perfectly calm. At last, a red shirt was thrown over her shoulders and bosom in the name of the law which orders this sort of vestment in all cases of parricide. Her delicate hands were tied behind her with a hard, strong twine. She rose. The gate of the prison opened. She appeared between an executioner and a priest, in presence of an immense crowd, whose curious stupor frightened her. She fainted. Justice, then, took her in pity. A carriage was brought to convey her, to spare her some humiliations. But, having recovered her senses, she refused to step into it, and walked on to the scaffold with a composed, humble, but firm and repentant countenance, as one condemned by men, but pardoned by God. All wept and sighed around her. All followed mournfully, anxiously, when, suddenly, she stopped before a statue of the holy Virgin, which she had seen in a niche above the city gate. It was a moment of painful uneasiness to all. Priest, executioner, men of arms, by-standers, every one stopped, also, and looked at her with a solicitous pity. She knelt. A solemn, profound, religious silence prevailed on all sides. Heaven itself seemed to listen; and the air echoed this her last but truly sublime prayer.

"'Mother of Jesus! come, now, and prepare a sinful woman to die! Thou seest from above my humiliation! Look also at my grief! Bear testimony to my repentance, so that, through thy efficacious intercession, the blood which they are to spill, and which I give them willingly, may efface for ever my crime, of which I now publicly accuse myself! Grant that this ignominious death, which I offer as an atonement for my depravity, may justify me when I appear before thy merciful son Jesus, whose innocent blood was shed for the reconciliation of sinners. I leave this earth which I have polluted, with the hope of a pardon from God in heaven.'

"Five minutes after, a large wicker basket spotted with blood carried off the mangled limbs and severed head of the lady. The priest blessed those disgusting remains of grandeur and beauty; prayed for the soul which had left them, and went home with a sorrowful heart, whilst the crowd dispersing slowly, took their way back to the city in which the remembrance of this sad and horrible drama will never perish."

87. I do not ask whether capital punishment should have been inflicted in such a case. It is evident that the murderess desired it as a favour. But did the law obtain, through her execution, the results which it intended? No, most certainly. Vengeance, however just it may be, is of no profit whatever for the avenger, when the individual whom it strikes is

changed, by a superior power, into an object of admiration for mankind, and a motive of forgiveness, nay, of blessing for heaven.—And it is a spectacle truly odious, when we see human justice pursuing with an instrument of death a being whom Divine justice consents to take in mercy!

88. Then, in any case, whether the convict be a remorseless villain, a perfidious hypocrite, an unfortunate innocent, an insane person or a repenting wretch, capital punishment is frustrated of such effects as are intended by the law. It can neither humiliate nor make the victim better. On the contrary, it either corresponds with the criminal desires of a few, or becomes an occasion of martyrdom for some others. It hurts the public feeling by its brutality towards consummated rogues or abused innocence, when it is not disappointed in its expectations by Heaven, which inspires guilt with a beneficial regret. It leaves horror where it was its purpose to heap humiliation, or bestows a scandalous notoriety where it pretended to inflict a dreadful infamy. Let who will speak of its merits, as for me, I cannot see them!

89. And, whereas, I have demonstrated above, that this sort of punishment encroaches upon the rights of God, that it sacrifices to an useless thirst of blood, and a vain idea of retaliation, the material interests of such persons as are to suffer directly by the results of a murder, that it is a mere remnant of barbarity left inadvertently in the law book of Christian civilization, I think I may safely conclude that it is a disgrace upon society, and ask for its abolition!

90. But, behold some of its most zealous supporters! They stand yet, some by the gallows, others by a *guillotine*, and beg that one be retained at least as a preventive remedy, if not as a means of correction. They say: Suppose that capital punishment produces no effect as regards the convict, you must still use it for the purpose of inspiring a salutary terror to villains, and diminishing the number of

capital crimes.—But this is, in my opinion, another error of the human mind.

91. Murder is the result of a perverted habit, which some have endeavoured to explain through a phrenological demonstration, and others through the unhappy development of a vicious education, whilst most part of men account for it by uttering the usual *I do not know*, which answers every doubt, every intricate question in favour of stupidity or tyranny. But in any way we choose to expound this awful crime, we must always come to this conclusion, that it is the effect either of a monomania which proceeds from a defect in the brain, if not from an imperceptible habit which grows in man without his knowledge until it has become irresistible, or of a tyrannical passion excited by certain circumstances which it is not in his power either to foresee, or to control at the time it rages in his mind. Now, can capital punishment, because a criminal suffers by it, be a preventive remedy against these infirmities of our nature?—I believe it not.

92. Whatever may our efforts be to instruct men and make them better, we have necessarily to meet in society with some extraordinary beings upon whom neither reason nor fear can operate efficaciously, who never will be either restrained by the horror of vice, nor attracted by the beauty of virtue. Religion and benevolence have proved to be useless to them. How could a criminal law better them? In no way, I am sure. They remain bad in spite of the pious hopes of a zealous clergy, and of the philosophical essays of an active philanthropy. Political as well as Christian civilization are both at a loss here. And why?—Because society cannot be better off on this score, than its divine Author chooses it to be. Like him, it goes spreading benefits, and like him, meets often in its way with vile insults and diabolical opposition. Such is its destiny on earth, that some will make use of the gifts which it bestows upon them only to afflict it;

whilst others will avail themselves of the means of safety with which it provides them, to disturb its repose and break its laws.—Depravity has crept, we do not know how, into the very heart of our race. We can restrain its influence, but we cannot destroy it entirely; and there it will remain, as long as God, who alone can do away with it, tolerates it in consequence of a design which we cannot penetrate.

93. Look at that man who leads a flagitious life!—There is no doubt but he receives from heaven such succours as he stands in need of to overpower the impulse of evil in his mind. However, he listens to it, caresses it, feeds upon it as it were, and lets it pervade gradually his very veins and bones.—Now, raise before him a scaffold! kill upon it a murderer! and say, so does justice treat all assassins!—Do you think that such a spectacle and speech will stop him in his career? Not at all.—By dint of conversing with his base inclinations, he has finished by obeying them blindly, and made of crime a companion with whom he is delighted to live. He considers it as a means of success, laughs at the awful consequences which may follow it, and, sooner or later, will risk his life in presence of your scaffolds as fearlessly as an honest warrior would expose his before the cannon of an enemy on the field of battle.—The examples drawn from a few villains who have turned honest men, prove no more against this habitual tendency of flagitiousness, than the conversion of a scandalous sinner on his death bed can prove against this truth founded upon practice, viz. that impious and unbelieving persons die, for the most part, as they have lived, in their impiety and incredulity. They serve only to show that our nature is susceptible, from time to time, of wonderful changes within, as it is, occasionally, susceptible of the most extraordinary forms without.—But the universal incontrovertible fact remains the same. Out of a hundred cases, depravity accomplishes its ends, as incredulity does its own, ninety-nine times. The bad propensities of the hu-

man heart as well as the whims of the human mind are habitually untractable. Threats, reasonings, sermons, are of no avail there.—Christ himself, whose views were so deep and correct, whose knowledge of man was so perfect, so astonishing that his very adversaries have been obliged to confess that he spoke like a God, Christ has acknowledged this sad propensity to evil in our kind, and said that it was an unconquerable neoessity. *Necesse est ut veniant scandala.—Oportet hæreses esse.*—Certainly, in the mind of those who worship him as a God, these two sentences must pass as an undeniable principle, and I will say to them: That man who dares to brave God, will mock society, and He who fears not hell will laugh at a scaffold!—Let men who think calmly take this argument into consideration! Let them meditate duly upon the decision brought by our Lord with regard to that mysterious necessity of crime as well as of impiety, *scandala* and *hæreses!* Let them see how much God is offended in consequence of it, and tell me, if they dare, why society should presume to do away with depravity?—We must not confound the right which we have of restraining evil, with the power which we have not of destroying its principle, and still less assume this power under the specious pretence that we use it but to restrain the wicked and hinder them from becoming worse.—But if capital punishment cannot be an efficacious remedy to prevent murders, why should we use it in preference to another that can restrain as well and chastise more severely, I mean hard labour and confinement!

94. But, if capital punishment, in spite of all the horrors which accompany it, cannot cause a hardened villain to deviate from his criminal course, still less will it have the intended effect upon a man who lives according to the laws of reason and justice! We never dread what we have no motive to be afraid of. However, every man carries along with him his passions, for which he cannot always answer.

I read, in the Confessions of the celebrated Augustine, bishop of Hippona, in Africa, that he would, every evening, thank God not only for the good actions which he had performed, but also for the grace which had hindered him from committing bad ones; and the reason which he gave for making such a prayer, was, that he knew not why he had not stolen, fornicated, killed, like many others, whilst he was not naturally better than any of them and bore, like them, in his heart all the passions which may cause the loss of a man, both in this world and in the other.—Let us remember, that many men have finished upon a scaffold, a life passed amidst the practices of virtue, up to the hour in which a single moment of forgetfulness precipitated them into the abyss of crime, and we will easily understand how philosophical that prayer of Augustine was!

95. No man can tell to-day what he may do to-morrow. Many who rise from their beds perfectly free, may sleep in a dungeon on the following night. One will kill his like just as another will fall into vice, at the very time he least expects it; for, very often, the loss of virtue, and the life of a man depend upon a sudden passion, an unguarded moment. Then, the dread of a scaffold cannot be more powerful than the fear of a reputation for ever blemished, to deter one from crime. As long as we are unaware of a passion which may lead us to infamy, we cannot guard against its inward progress; and when it bursts out suddenly, its force is so violent that we see nothing but what our desires show us.

96. Undoubtedly, man has to atone for any crime which he commits; and his crime is more or less punishable, according to its greater or lesser intensity, which men determine commonly by examining attentively all its contingencies: but, whatever may that unexpected crime be, we cannot deny that it is derived from a passion which is also a mere contingency. Now, as such a contingency does not enter habitually into what we term very properly the cal-

culation of human probabilities, I ask how capital punishment can—I will not say prevent, but annihilate that contingency? Certainly it cannot.

97. Such passions as may expose us to an ignominious death are, by no means, similar to those which may cause us to deserve imprisonment. They are differently conceived, and set into operation through another principle than common wickedness. Unless the power of virtue, directed by an influence from above, restrains them, they rush forth like the stormy waves of an irritated sea, which yield to no other obstacle but an immense, deep-founded rock, against which they break, helter-skelter, and exhaust, at last, their tumultuous rage. Men may write and talk as much as they please upon this grave and important topic; but facts speak a language which cannot be refuted. In spite of every reasoning to prove the contrary, violent passions will go on until they are satisfied: it is their natural bent never to stop but when their work is completed, and when the man who performs it has either to rejoice or to shudder at their consequences. I wish that lawgivers would understand this! When they do, they will confess also that capital punishment is no preventive remedy in such cases.

98. No one can doubt that a good criminal code is of the utmost importance to society; as, in many instances, it will inspire mischievous people with a salutary fright. Were it not for fear of being sent to a penitentiary, many whom we call gentlemen, would commit rape, incest, adultery, steal, counterfeit, swindle, disturb in different ways the repose of the community. So, whereas the community inflicts infamy upon those who are punished for these various offences, it is from this cause that many avoid committing them. Hence the advantage of the criminal law. Considered under this light it is moral, salutary; it is a preventive. But it is not so, when it kills a man to prevent others from spilling blood unjustly. It chastises the guilty, but does not

eradicate the propensity to crime. It avenges, as we say, social order, but does not save it from further violation. Nothing is so easy to say as that the gallows represses rascality; but it is impossible to name those whom it has actually restrained from crime. The fear which hinders a man from murdering another, is evidently the effect of religion or of virtue, which, however small it is, exercises upon his mind all the power which some dare to attribute to a bloody machine put in motion to kill murderers legally. When I study the annals of society, I find that the number of villains who expose themselves to this sort of punishment, has been commonly the same every where. It seems that Providence which permits crime, has, on the other hand, marked its limits. It shall not pass them.

99. The arguments which some philosophers are pleased to bring as a peremptory answer to my objections, are, methinks, as defective as those which certain divines draw from the shame which one has in confessing his sins. However eloquent such arguments may be, they fail completely, for example, in our criminal courts and Catholic confessionals; for in both places the judge and the priest have always, the one, crimes of the same nature to punish, the other, faults of the same kind to correct. It is a fact that man commits evil, when his passions control him, without caring much about the consequences, and then, endeavours either to avoid the punishment of the law, or obtain absolution from the church. Let us speak of virtue and divine grace as being preventive remedies! I believe they are. But let us be persuaded that a bloody punishment is but an act of brutal force which shows the impotence and not the morality of a government.

100. I need not, most assuredly, to reason long, in order to demonstrate that the gallows is of no use to restrain maniacs. Murder, which is the business of a bandit, is an action without a certain motive in

an insane person. Whilst the former meets the scaffold without shuddering, since he had it always in view, the latter will either cry like a child or laugh like a fool, when they place him upon the fatal boards. Therefore, you may burn, hang, or behead assassins as much as you please in his presence; but your severity will not cause his thoughts or feelings to change. What does it matter him if you dip in blood your social cloak? What does he understand, when you talk of law, of police, of criminal courts? Nothing. For him, liberty consists not in submitting to social order, but in obtaining, no matter how, what he wishes for. He will never stop, but when he has seen the object of his folly, seized it, destroyed it. From this you may learn, ye wise legislators, that law is no authority when reason fails.

CONCLUSION.

Such is my opinion upon capital punishment. It was but after a long, conscientious inquiry into its motives and consequences, that I decided to unite with many other philanthropists, in favour of its abolition. Study and experience have always accompanied me, from the moment in which I began this disquisition up to the last word in it. Though I profess a sincere respect for the religious opinions of men, and excuse the many prejudices of legislators, I am, however, no slave to either. My only desire is to render to God what I owe him, that is to say, adoration, submission to his decrees, and a love as pure as possible. In regard to men, I see them in God, and no where else. What I do for them is the result of my belief in God, and of my obedience to his law, which breathes in me as in other men, naturally. So, if I have appeared rather severe towards some of them, I wish it to be understood, that I was so, less through a spirit of bitter criticism, than through zeal for the rights of heaven and reason. All that seemed rational to me in our modern legislation, I have defended honestly, but all that I thought to be a mere usurpation of the celestial power, should, vice versa, be discussed freely by me. My main idea is, that God alone has an unlimited power over our lives. I consider it as an undeniable truth. Hence all my reasonings, and all the facts by which I have endeavoured to illustrate them! That I am not infallible, I confess most humbly, but I firmly believe, also, that I am right in all that I have said, and will persevere in my belief, until some one convinces me that I am wrong.

Let justice, therefore, be rendered to my thoughts! Let any person who says that our Bible must become the standard of legislation, or that the law of nature authorizes judicial murder, come forth and argue fairly with me! I will wait for him quietly within that rational circle which an upright philosophy has traced for all philanthropic inquiries. A thorough investigation, the object of which should be to ascertain whether God allows men to keep scaffolds and executioners, will not fail to interest the community, without the decision of which, no one can know which of the two arguments may be correct.

Until then, I submit my opinion to such of my readers as will be pleased to examine it, and I claim no other favour but that of an impartial judgment. Whatever may their previous impressions be, let them be aware, when they have perused my book, that it is the fruit of a long, serious and unprejudiced meditation, which I have often resumed, not in my room, amidst many other philosophical speculations, but in the many dungeons which I have visited either as a sincere believer in the Christian faith, or as a practical friend of social order. A profound knowledge of the motives and effects of crime, which I have acquired through several condemned criminals whom I have been allowed to see before their execution, and a painful remembrance of several facts which I have witnessed, either in their solitary cell or on the scaffold, where they ended miserably their wicked career, are the only reasons which I have to give to justify the publication of my views upon a subject so grave, and the authorities upon which I exposed them.

Every man should acquire, within the sphere which he has chosen, an experience which exists not in those who happen to be differently situated, and which they must, of course, admit as a practical rule of conduct. Hence those consultations, or committees properly so styled, artistical, medical, military, commercial, legislative, or academical, according to the profession of those citizens who compose them, and whose decisions are, consequently, adopted as laws with regard to such matters as have been discussed by them respectively!

Why, then, should not society appoint a committee, whose business it would be to call crime to their bar, to investigate its causes and results, and to decide upon the best way of having it duly punished. Their decision, if we suppose it is that of proper judges, would be serviceable to society, so far as there is no doubt but they would free it from the shameful and degrading task of looking out among its members to find a judicial murderer, a regular hangman. The stamp of infamy, which is impressed by the community on the face of such a character, or the disgraceful disguise which he is obliged to assume in those places where the criminal law, ashamed of its barbarity, allows a sheriff to hire a mercenary hand, that he may spill the blood of a man legally condemned, without spotting his own hands with it, and smelling of the scaffold when he enters society, speaks clearly enough to make us understand that, in reality, capital punishment is not less horrid than murder itself; nay, that the man who inflicts it is still more abhorred than the one upon whom it is inflicted.

The sight of a murderer inspires either fright or compassion; but the presence of an executioner spreads around him horror and disgust. Honest people will consent to live with an assassin in a case of necessity, but they never would dwell in the same house with an executioner, though this one kills for the profit of a law which the other has violated. Then, what is, in fact, a form of legislation, or rather a law which renders the public avenger of crime more odious than crime itself! And when shall we do away with this only remnant of barbarous cruelty among us? Have we no other means of safety against murderers than a hangman; and can we not punish them efficaciously but with an axe, a wheel, or a rope? I answer this important question by stating simply, that a system of public instruction, well conducted, is a surer preventive than a cruel law; and that a jail well kept, is a punishment more rational than death.

Whilst I was consulting attentively the annals of crime, I had often an occasion to notice that murder never was the work of ignorance. It requires, I may say, a certain development of intellect, of which a simpleton is not susceptible, and it is more or less horrid in its circumstances, according to the greater or lesser degree of knowledge which the murderer may have reached previously. Indeed, so far as I know, no one is to be found who is not eloquent when he attempts to defend the cause of crime, or whose repentance is not really sublime, when he makes a confession of his wickedness; and I dare to conclude from my investigations, that depravity is, as well as virtue, the source of a true, inward-felt elocution.

Then, in order to restrain men from committing crime, society should oppose such passions as may lead to it, by teaching such virtues as can impress a salutary horror of all that is bad, injurious to others, and contrary to social order. Moderation, honesty, submission, patience, condescension and disinterestedness should be fostered by lawgivers, and made practical by our civil administrations. But how can all this be done by society, and where is the source of all these virtues? This question is more difficult to answer than that above, because all men do not agree upon its solution.

Some think that philosophy, as it is taught to us by nature, and explained by the honest writers of all times and nations, should be the only principle of social virtue. Others pretend that it should be religion, wisely mixed with social legislation. Both parties, no doubt, are impelled by the purest motives, but both may mistake by adhering too exclusively to their respective notions. Philosophy opens, I believe, a measureless field to politics. By securing a perfect freedom of thought to all, it leaves room to the most contradictory notions; and such has become the absolutism of individuality through it, as to render it impossible for two philosophers to agree on every point.—Who would admit, as the main principle of public morals, that right which every man should have to oppose his fellow beings mentally! Indeed, Theocracy, whilst it addresses men in the name of God, seems to have a decided advantage over philosophy: but if it promises to better mankind by gathering them together within the same pale, and endeavouring to inspire them with one faith, common to all; it is, however, defective, so far as it takes, in the hands of men, a thousand forms, the effect of which is to divide, and to force, if not to oppress, by dividing.—Means of this kind may be as dangerous for some as it will prove useful for others, and, therefore, cannot be chosen as a standard for civil morality! Religion and nature agree together; nothing is more certain: but priests and philosophers are, by no means, the one better than the other, to govern society. Whilst the latter authorize men to think freely, Impiety and libertinism, the ordinary fruit of science ill-digested, may prevail; and the former, by leading their disciples into mysticism, may, though unwillingly, teach them to be egotistical, fanatical, persecuting tyrants. Most assuredly, both results are great evils; and, consequently, another mode of improving public morals must be looked for. What may it be?

I will not be positive in my assertion, but I dare to say that it should be such as to combine well together the various elements which constitute society, and operate so as Theocracy, or, in other words, the church may, through charity and unity wisely preached, secure the state against anarchy; and Philosophy or natural inspiration shelter it, through a prudent opposition, from every ecclesiastical usurpation. Then, the philosophical idea, ruling by a rational majority, would enact laws without being answerable for them to the church; and the theocratical thought, made uniform in matters of morals, though it varies in matters of doctrine, could act easily in accordance with its object, and be altogether independent of the law. In a word, it is desirable that, like the grand master of both philosophy and theocracy, Jesus Christ, society would render to God his due on the one side, and on the other, preserve its own rights untouched.

The religion of Christ is not admissible as a principle of legislation. He has said so himself: *My kingdom is not of this world.* But, so far as it is considered as a means of civilization, no one can doubt its excellence. Should certain of his modern apostles consent to divest his heavenly doctrines of the many vain ornaments with which their predecessors thought proper to robe them during former ages, and would offer them to men, such as they were taught by Christ himself, with no other view than to render them as profitable to the human heart as they are admirable to the human mind, I entertain no doubt but that these doctrines would triumph over the world. When that takes place, Jesus will enjoy all the privileges which his divinity expects from men; society will better itself; virtue will reign, and crime, of course, be diminished.

Diminished, I say, but not destroyed; for it is not in our power to do away with it altogether. When we have succeeded so far as to oppose a real, positive obstacle to villany, we should be satisfied. An impartial justice is all that is left to us when the voice of virtue has proved to be of no avail; and the task of that justice should be fulfilled scrupulously. It is, I confess, a painful, but necessary task. Then, let society stand between a temple and a jail! And if it happens that the oracles of the former are despised, with regard to such laws as are enacted for the sake of society, let the cells of the latter be opened to receive the offender! Thus does the omnipotent God dispense justice from the throne which he occupies on the confines of this life and of the next.

Seated there, in all his glory, and assisted by Truth, his eternal companion, he summons mankind; and, as they appear before him, he condemns or rewards them according to their deeds; permits those to enter who have obeyed his instructions, and dooms to an everlasting imprisonment all those who have resisted his grace and rejected his favours.

Society, I think, cannot imitate a better example. In the same manner as a man who is found guilty before the tribunal of his Divine Author, has nothing else to expect but an after-life of misery, the extent of which shall be in a due proportion to the gravity of his offence or his contempt for the religious law, so the citizen who has offended society, and despised such of its moral ordinances as must be observed under the penalty of a corresponding chastisement for every infraction of them, should be condemned to imprisonment only, society having a care to modify his sufferings so as to render them more or less painful, according to the greater or lesser intensity of his depravity. When a court of justice has condemned him, let the iron door of a penitentiary be closed upon him, either for life or for a time only; and when he is there separated from honest people, let silence and hard labour teach him gradually, that the only tie which may unite him now with society is a firm and severe justice! Perhaps God will enlighten his mind and touch his heart, either by himself or through the charity of a priest, of a philanthropist or some other person whom His Spirit may be pleased to use as an instrument; for, if men cannot usurp the power of God, they are, however, entitled to give good counsel and help the cause of virtue.

This remark leads me to investigate a mode of punishment which seems to have become a serious topic for philanthropy; I mean solitary confinement! There is no doubt that by isolating convicts from each other in a prison, society has improved its system of criminal justice. Besides the many humiliations which a prisoner is free from, and thereby saved from a thousand occasions of growing more depraved, for humiliated criminals become mortal foes of virtue; he is also placed in a condition, the sadness of which forces him to enter his conscience, and, occasionally, to accuse himself, to repent, and to vow sincerely a better course of life, as his solitude dispenses him with that scandalous brotherhood which never unites villains in a jail where they are shut up together but to oblige them to a criminal partnership when they meet again in society.

But is it practically true that solitary confinement produces upon the minds of convicts such good effects as are intended by the law? Is it practically true that the absolute silence of a cell will destroy vice, and spin on the wheel of grief, if I can say so, the tissue of a virtuous life? There are men who believe, and others who deny it. Without pretending to decide between the two parties, I would say that inasmuch as its results may correspond with the hopes of society, solitary confinement is, undoubtedly, an excellent invention; but, whereas the expectations of its inventors have been, often, deceived, I should also conclude that it is, in some manner, defective, and requires, of course, a certain modification, at least with regard to such convicts as are condemned to it for a long period of years.

It is crime, I believe, but not the rational affections of man, which the law is bound to punish; and society, by isolating a convict too rigorously, may do him as much harm as it will do good to those from whom he is thus separated: for, whilst he is physically impeded from committing evil, he is also deprived of many means of amendment. Why should we deprive him of seeing some of those honest people of whom he was once an acquaintance; his family, whose existence has been poisoned by his villany; his children, whose name he has dishonoured; in a word, all such persons as may cause him to regret the past, and deplore the desolating effects of his unruled passions! That studied hypocrisy which a solitary confinement suggests to a convict whose imprisonment is limited, may be changed into an abyss of despair, the depth of which extends far beyond the human reach, when it enters the mind of another whose imprisonment is to last for ever. The thought that the feelings of his family and former friends towards him shall never be known by him again, that he shall see no more those who might have taken some interest in his unhappy fate, nor be able to ascertain whether they pity him, and believe that he repents, this only thought, I say, may overwhelm his mind, rend his heart, irritate his conscience, and make him doubt his God. The jailer who watches by his cell, the turnkey who brings him a poor pittance, the clergyman who hopes to convert him, and even the conversations of the philanthropist, inspire him commonly, with no other feeling than that of a deplorable mistrust. He looks at them as a thief yet at large will look at any person whom he suspects and takes for a police officer. He listens and answers, not because he is pleased to talk with that class of visiters, but because he must obey under the awful vault which bends over him, and seems to force his head to lower before the merciless regulation of a cell. So, none of those persons who are strangers to him, and whom, therefore, he is always inclined to consider as mere spies, can awake in his heart such good impressions as are supposed to exist virtually in a solitary cell! But, let him be approached by those who are still dear to him, whom he cannot help considering as an essential part of himself, and whose life is made unhappy by his! Then, his mind will be inspired with profitable thoughts, and his heart feel deeply. Earth being yet something for him, it will lead him to regard heaven with less indifference. The cup of sorrow which justice has filled to quench his criminal thirst will not be so bitter to drink, and instead of being so intoxicated by its contents as to be incapable of thinking, he will sip it leisurely, and resign himself to his fate. The hard labour imposed upon him will become a consolation amidst his remorse; he will accept it as a means of expiation, acknowledge the justice of your severity by his submission, wet his couch with the tears of repentance during his moments of rest; and his death, when God judges proper to take him from this world, will leave no doubt in the mind of society with regard to the efficacy of its criminal law.

The murderer, upon whom a solitary confinement thus combined with humanity cannot produce a salutary change, is not a man, but a demon, obstinately waring against heaven. Society has not to repent for having buried him alive in a dungeon! But if another avails himself of such a chastisement so as to conclude amicably with God the unlucky affair which made him incur justly the enmity of mankind, let society congratulate itself for this new invention! It is wonderful.

And, what is to be done to have solitary confinement thus improved? A little more trouble on the part of the jailer. Let the jailer never introduce to his prisoner but such persons as are well known for their excellent morality, and whose visits can help the charitable intent of the law; and let the turnkeys stand at such a distance as they may easily interfere if there is an occasion for it! Every precaution must be taken to secure the convict; but when men adopt a punishment through a spirit of true philanthropy, that same spirit should remove every obstacle that may cheat its hopes, and order all the means that may insure it success. Certainly I ask nothing else here but what the study of the law of nature has suggested before to any man who has taken the trouble of analyzing carefully all its principles!—On another hand, society has sanctioned the right of pardoning with which its executive is commonly invested. But what is that right, if not a practical acknowledgment of the hope of amendment which society is pleased to entertain when it punishes? And if it is so, why hesitate to take every moral means which may facilitate that amendment, and, through it, justify a pardon? I know that some philosophers who agree with me on this point of public morals, viz: that capital punishment should be abolished, would refuse society the right of pardoning; but it seems that, by refusing it, they contradict themselves. Since the amendment of the convict with regard to what he owes God, is of no direct use to us, I do not understand a severity the object of which should be to continue chastising for ever a man who has, at last, answered its expectations, and upon the future honesty of whom society may depend.

Such a man who seems to be incorrigible, thinks, perhaps, of becoming better. Whether a sudden inspiration from above enlightens his intellect amidst its flagitious plots, as it was the case with Paul on the road to Damascus, or a secret and almost irresistible feeling touches his heart, and frees it from the most contemptible passions, as it happened to Augustine under a fig tree, man passes, sometimes, from an awful state of depravity to a sincere love of virtue.

I have heard of a hermit, who died amidst the blessings and regrets of all those who knew him, and whom he had edified by his penance during twenty-three years, though he had spent his youth amidst every sort of crimes, and had escaped the hand of an executioner, almost miraculously. His history is worth reading; and I will tell it as it was related to me by a monk of the Mount St. Bernard, who assisted him in his last moments.

"He was born of a noble and wealthy family in France. Pleasing hopes of future grandeur and honour smiled on his cradle. His childhood was gay and promising. Every one at home lavished kisses and caresses upon him. Had heaven continued to bless his native land, he would have lived to see many glorious and happy days.

"But, whilst he was yet a boy, God permitted a frightful revolution to ravage France. Government, religion, order, all were destroyed. Princes, priests, nobles, rich and poor were proscribed, arrested and put to death; streams of blood ran where honour was proverbial, and a few tyrants changed into a den of ferocious beasts the very sanctuary in which the law, incorruptible protector of equity, should have always reigned.

"Then, every prospect of peace and happiness was taken away. Each one trembled for himself; the laws of nature were trampled upon; every day saw new crimes perpetrated; parents were snatched from the arms of their children, and immolated to a restless fury which boasted of erecting its horrible throne upon dead bodies and ruins. Almost all those who were unable to escape, perished miserably, and left their little ones destitute and exposed to a legal contempt, by their confiscated estates and their polluted tombs.

"Now, it happened that N . . . . . was one of those who found themselves thus abandoned, and reduced to the utmost misery, in consequence of the untimely death of their parents, and of the sanguinary covetousness of their tyrannical masters. His father, mother, and two sisters had been beheaded, and he had been turned out mercilessly from his house and estate, which were given to the man who had denounced his family and caused his poverty.

"As he was too young, then, to comprehend how cruel an offence he had received, he had nothing to oppose but his cries and tears, and went with his nurse into a cottage, where the charity of the poor was his only resource. But, two years of pain and sorrow having elapsed, he grew stronger, and felt much more how wretched his condition was. He inquired about his parents, and learnt their tragical end, how he had lost by their death, every hope of maintaining the same honourable standing his ancestors bore in society, and what a train of misfortunes had been bequeathed to him by the infamous murderers of those whose life would have made his happiness. He quaked with horror, hearing of such atrocities, and hatred and revenge, two passions nearly excusable, when they spring from such injuries as those which he had endured, entered violent and resolute in his outraged soul. He swore he would die rather than not fight the monsters who had butchered his family, and started to enlist himself amongst the heroes, who were then warring in Vendée against the troops of the French convention.

"As long as the Vendean phalanxes maintained the contest with advantage, he was celebrated for his valour, and deserved, on many occasions, military honours; but, when several defeats had forced to a despairing submission those provinces which had opposed vigorously the republican government, and when, therefore, he had no more a chance of satisfying his anger without running the risk of loosing his good character, he was incensed at a truce which put an end to all his hopes of vengeance; and, determined to war, right or wrong, against an authority which he hated, he left the honourable career of a soldier to join a band of young men who, dissatisfied as he was, had organized a sort of an association, the object of which was to stop the mail, rob the public money, and even plunder the houses of civil officers. Their pretence was, that they might attack tyrants who had attacked and enslaved their country; but their mode of waring was indeed that of a set of banditti armed against social order, for the bloody legislation of Paris had ceased at that time, and better days seemed to have come in France.

"At first, that band succeeded in almost all its enterprises. The unsettled state of the country, the uncertainty of an ever-changing administration, and, especially, the depravity of the many leaders who had contended among themselves to obtain the supreme power, were as many licenses granted to highway robbers, who availed themselves of those unhappy circumstances. Crime was considered rather as an act of courage and honour, and those who perpetrated it boasted publicly of its terrible consequences. So true it is that vice triumphs among such nations as have neglected to respect virtue! Depraved politicians could not oppose efficaciously rogues who laughed at every measure which was ordered to put a check to their plundering; their success blinded them; they thought themselves great when they were but criminal; and their new companion, deceived both by their unjust triumphs and their dangerous principles, had finished by believing that he was a hero when he was but a rascal.

"However, his true position was at last ascertained; for, as soon as the political equilibrium of France had been restored, and the power fallen into the hands of one great man, Napoleon, severe ordinances were issued to secure the public peace, stop malefactors of all denominations, and render every communication easy between the capital and the provinces. The band to which N. . . . . belonged was especially threatened; and he who presumed to be honourable in spite of his misdeeds, saw himself now considered as an outlaw, stamped with the seal of infamy, pursued as a murderer, and doomed to perish ignominiously upon a scaffold. This awful change in his condition should have caused him to reflect and become a good citizen in a country where the law had resumed its empire. On the contrary, he felt more irritated by this circumstance, and took with some others the sacrilegious oath which bound him to continue his life of a vagabond. Neither the sight of the scaffold upon which many of his companions had perished in Lyons, nor the shame which awaited him if he should fall into the hands of justice, could deter him from his bad purpose. When the band of robbers to which he belonged had been dispersed, he entered a gang of *Chauffeurs*, monsters in human frames, whose thirst for blood and rapine caused, for a time, all France to shudder.

"These wretched men had laid their plundering hands upon the whole country. Aided by a counter-police, which they maintained both in large cities, and even among the officers of the crown, they never were to be found in such places as they were supposed to be. They entered, at night, the castles and farm-houses, and surprised, by their sudden and frightful appearance, their owners and inmates, stifled their cries by gagging them, tied their hands, chained their legs, and then burned their feet, either by means of redhot iron plates or by dipping them in boiling oil, until the unfortunate victims of their barbarous cruelty consented to give them whatever treasures they possessed.

"Undoubtedly, the man whose history I relate, would contract the horrid habit of shedding blood, if he associated with such banditti; for naturally proud and ambitious, he would not have remained in the rear. Always ready to distinguish himself among his like, and jealous of an uncontrovertible superiority, he fell gradually into the deepest abyss of flagitiousness. There was no crime, however revolting, he would hesitate to commit. Neither age nor sex was respected by him; children, old people, women, all had to suffer by him. The most atrocious libertinism, united in him with an incredible covetousness of riches and thirst of blood; rarely would he steal or murder, without adding some other atrocities to his original crime. One might have said of him, what the prophet king says of a reprobate, that he wrapped himself up in malediction, allowed crime to enter his heart and mind, caused depravity to run through his veins and nerves like oil runs through all the threads of a cloth upon which one lets it fall, and permitted evil to drag him into the abyss of perdition, as a torrent, falling from the summit of a perpendicular rock, sweeps off into the chasm beneath every thing that opposes its course. However, the hour of vengeance was about to strike. The hands of justice surprised him amidst his deeds of blood; they led him to prison, threw him into a dungeon, loaded him with heavy fetters, judged him promptly, and he was sentenced to die on a scaffold, not as an innocent victim of that revolution of which the nefarious authors had murdered his respectable parents, but as a vile wretch justly cursed and justly punished.

"Every one abhorred him. The earth seemed to shake under him, and to refuse receiving his doomed body; the pangs of his conscience caused him more remorse than public vituperation, and his crimes weighed so heavy upon him, that he had not strength enough either to despair or to repent. Like that impious giant who had dared to brave heaven, and whom heaven kept a prisoner under a mountain, he could neither move, speak, nor even sigh. All those who were, then, admitted to see him, believed that he was equally cursed by God and man, and that the reprobation which had struck him on earth, was to last for ever in the other world. They spoke but of his execution, and all prepared to see him die and pass from the grasp of a bloody executioner into that of hell, though they could not help pitying his fate.

"But Heaven, which is often pleased to impugn the judgments of men, and disappoint the world in its expectations, touched the heart of that man at the very time when the earth was about to cast him off, and hell was open to receive him. The voice of religion which he had despised so long, produced upon his faculties, seemingly absorbed by crime, and buried in infamy, the most wonderful effect. He lent to the sacred words of Jesus, which a priest uttered piously by his side, an attentive ear; turned his eyes to heaven; rose slowly from his damp couch of straw like a pale spectre from the tomb; looked around him as if to interrogate those deep mysteries of iniquity into which he had fallen so terribly; knelt fervently before a crucifix which a charitable hand presented him; heaved painfully from his exhausted breast a long heart rending sob; joined convulsively his hands; and let, at last, escape from his parched lips, these words of remorse and repentance: Oh, God! good Good! have mercy on me!... Then, the priest had but to listen and shudder, for the confession of so many crimes, the horrors of which surpassed all that he had heard or even imagined of human ferocity, was made aloud by their repentant author, whose conscience seemed to breathe more freely in proportion as it disclosed its hideous secrets.

"But whilst his confession revealed the monstrous excesses of which a ruthless depravity is capable, his repentance and grief were as sincere and as consoling to see as his guilt had been enormous and shocking. He shed abundant tears; struck his breast with a frenzied violence; cursed mercilessly his criminal passions; implored with a beseeching voice the forgiveness of men and the pity of God; rolled himself like a madman on the pavement of his cell; despaired of ever obtaining mercy from heaven; besought his Saviour to rid him of the dreadful phantoms which, he said, pursued him, night and day; asked for his life, that he might have time to repent and expiate amidst tortures his numberless crimes.

"Then, recovering his senses, and passing in review all his past life, he seemed to doubt whether he was really the son of an honest man, scrutinized minutely all his iniquities the one after the other, blushed, grew pale, dejected, finally enraged again, and fell senseless on his irons, the rattling of which caused all the prison to echo the mournful toll of death. Divine and earthly justice had never met before with such an awful sight!

"And that unfortunate being, placed as he was between them, never ceased to invoke the former, begging with an artless and hopeful fervour to be freed from the pitiless wrath of the latter. The scaffold appeared not to him a punishment too severe, for he acknowledged that he had deserved it a thousand times, but he dreaded to perish upon it. His conscience overwhelmed with remorse admitted that infamy should be its frightful lot, and he demanded to suffer, provided it were not by the hands of an executioner. Had they opened before him a dungeon, in which tribulations and punishments of every description would have combined together for the purpose of incessantly torturing all his senses, he would have precipitated himself into it eagerly and thanked men for the opportunity which they gave him to atone duly and fully for his crimes. But, to ascend publicly a scaffold, to be exposed there to the bloody curiosity of an infuriated mob, and have his head cut off by a degraded and filthy being, whose sullied hands would take it out from the disgusting bag into which it had to fall, and show it as an ignominious trophy of social revenge; to that he could not make up his mind, and all his thoughts tended to find a means of avoiding it, if heaven consented to let him do so.

"Thus, whilst the priest exhorted him, and thought that he was listening to the soothing voice of a religion made, it seems, to inspire guilt with confidence as much as with remorse, he dreamt only of acquiring his liberty, and contrived in his mind how he might effect his purpose, which he realized at last in the following manner:

"As the priest informed him that they would behead him on the next day, he borrowed from that charitable and pious man a watch, under the pretence of using it as a clock, the striking of which would apprize him of his coming end and keep him awake up to his last moment. But, as soon as he had got that long desired watch, he opened it, broke off its main spring of which he made a saw, and spent all the night in sawing his irons, but in such a manner that the jailer could not be aware of it on the morning when he would come and take him out of his dungeon to deliver him to the officers of justice who ought to bring him in the place where he had committed his last crime, and where, in pursuance with the sentence which weighed upon him, he was to be executed. Indeed, all went on as he had foreseen. The jailer wholly unconscious of his project, thought only of pitying him, and, without inspecting his irons, handed him over to the officers of justice, who threw him on a car between the priest and the executioner, and they made ready to start. But the attorney general ordered them to wait until sunset, lest the mob should follow and incumber the road, or, perhaps, cause a dangerous riot by taking justice in their own hands.

"Thus, it was very near dark when they departed. The priest continued praying to God and exhorting his penitent. The executioner smoked his pipe, now ascending and then descending the car for the slightest motive, and with that carelessness which none but an executioner can be susceptible of in such circumstances. The officers of justice, on their side, trusted the irons of the convict more than their sabres and pistols, and would now gallop and then trot or pace as they felt inclined. Night came. Thick clouds veiled a winter sky. A cold freezing blast blew from the north. The trees and hedges agitated by it filled the air with dreadful murmurs. Every one seemed to forget why he was there, and all conspired to facilitate the escape of the prisoner. He perceived it, and availing himself of the inexcusable remissness of his judicial foes, succeeded in liberating himself from his fetters. A smile of inconceivable joy breathed unseen on his silent lips. His eyes rest with a preternatural hope upon a dense forest which extended now along the road; he begs of Heaven to divert the attention of the executioner, who was now walking among the officers of police; looks with confidence at the priest, tells him that he has broken his chains, beseeches him to keep a discreet silence, slides through the rails of the car, jumps over a large ditch, enters the forest of which the most secret recesses are well known to him, and disappeared so suddenly that he was in a safe place before his escape had been noticed.

"In vain they beat the forest on every side, in vain all the neighbouring peasants arm themselves and run after him, in vain justice offers rewards for his apprehension, he has deceived them all, and the scaffold has lost its prey. Where has that villain gone, they say, where has he found a shelter? What hiding place secretes the criminal, who, notwithstanding his conversion, should have atoned before men for all the evils which he inflicted upon so many harmless and honest people? No doubt but he has either destroyed himself or joined another band of banditti. 'Will not justice succeed in recapturing him?

"So they spoke, but all were mistaken in their conjectures. The horror which the escaped convict felt for his crimes, was as sincere as his repentance was efficacious. By avoiding the scaffold, he intended not to free himself from sufferings. Whilst they went in every direction to discover his hiding place, he had gone to a monastery, where they thought not, of course, of asking for him.

"There only he had been able to enter fully within himself, and see the horrid state of his conscience. The hardships and severe penance to which he had submitted, seemed to him light, and too mild in comparison with those which he had imagined; and he had decided to add many other excruciating austerities to those which were ordered by the regulations of the convent; but Providence would not allow him such a favour.

"As soon as he had apprized the Superior of his flagitious life, that honest Monk told him candidly that the honour of the monastery obliged its Superior not to receive in it a fugitive from justice, and ordered him to leave it; advising him, at the same time, to go and look for a solitude in which he might undergo willingly, and far from his native country, such sufferings and chastisements as he would judge necessary to inflict upon himself in order to atone for his crimes in this world, and obtain a pardon from God in the other. This was a severe but indispensable command.

"So, the convict departed, filled both with the shame and remorse which raged in his mind and the fear of again falling into the hands of justice. As long as he trod on the French soil, he felt uneasy; the sight of a man caused him to shrink and shudder; his natal air suffocated him, and the land of his fathers refused to bear him: he thought he heard a a distant noise, which, as it gradually increased, sounded to him like the dreadful notes of those mysterious trumpets with which the angels of an omnipotent Judge will awake the dead, and call them out of their tombs to receive their everlasting sentence. The threatening fury of angry waves breaking against a sandy shore, which, unable to oppose their resistless force, is engulfed in their unfathomable depths, is but an imperfect image of all the terrors which besieged that wretched reprobate. Afraid both of God and of man, he neither dared to look to heaven nor to trust the earth. Obliged to hide himself during the day, he went on his way during the night, the darkness of which increased his fright. Hunger consumed him; but, rather than beg of a man a piece of bread, he sucked the roots of the trees, and devoured the grass left on the road side by the cattle. And he who, a few months before, would not have hesitated spilling blood to amass riches, was afraid now to pick up some grains and touch the fruits which he saw in the fields. Condemned to die on a scaffold, he would not commit a trifling theft to feed his exhausted body. Indeed, the mind and heart of man is a deep mystery!

"After much uneasiness and many fatigues, he arrived at last in a narrow valley, which was limited on the east and west by high mountains. He studied his position, and ascertained that he had entered one of the cantons of Switzerland. Content to be in a foreign country, and free from all judicial pursuit, at least as long as he should be unknown, he slackened his march, and letting his mind prey upon the past, followed the way along the river Rhone; of which the rapid and tumultuous current was a representation of the inward agitation which he experienced, and which hurried him down into the abyss of an infinite misery. Had he been able to remain there, for ever absorbed in his grief and an incessant prey to his remorse, he would have been satisfied, and awaited patiently the hour of death. But such is the destiny of guilt, as well as of virtue, that neither the one nor the other can live unoccupied.

"He proceeded, and entered the capital of the canton about dusk. At first, the sight of man brings back in his mind the fear of justice; he feels embarrassed amidst a population which knows him not;

he thinks that every one looks at him, reads in his face what passes in his heart, avoids and curses him. Who will give him a shelter? Who will let repose under an unsullied roof, a head which belongs to an executioner? Who will employ a murderer? Who will let him share even the litter of a horse in a stable? Who will allow a reprobate to enter the house of an honest family? Nobody. Every one rejects me, every one hates me, every one condemns me; I am poor and hungry, but I am also a villain whom nature abhors, and therefore they have no pity for me. Well! then let me die! .... And, saying so, he fell breathless on a stone, by the shop of a basket maker.

"Immediately a wondering crowd gathered around, the basket maker brought him into his shop, and gave him a drink, which recalled him to his senses. A tear of gratitude fell from his burning eyes; he stated to his benefactor how poor and destitute he was, begging him, in the name of God, to give him a shelter and procure him some work.

"The van maker, who was compassionate, consoled him, offered him a lodging in his house, and to share his pittance with him; and added, that he might compensate by his work whatever expense his coming in the family would cause. The bargain was good, and it was accepted, not on account of its pecuniary advantages by the convict, but for the purpose of learning a trade which he could follow in his solitude.

"Such was his application, that he soon gained the affection of his host, who admired both his improvement and the regularity of his conduct; he had pleased also all the inmates of the family by his constant attention to their wishes; his honesty was praised by every body, and he had become a model which every tradesman showed to his journeymen as the best which they could imitate. But his object was not to enjoy a reputation which a disclosure of his past life would infallibly destroy. He endeavoured, on the contrary, to remain unknown; the austerities which he used to practice, his sincere and exemplary religion, his ascetic life, which seemed to become every day dearer and more precious to him, his perfect submission and devout obedience towards his master, and, more especially, the strict silence which he observed, made him pass, among the neighbours, for a man who belonged no more to this world; so that no one was surprised when, at the end of a few months, he retired into a solitary spot he had discovered upon an almost inaccessible mountain.

"From the moment he settled there, he thought only of beginning a career of suffering and pain; all his time was spent in praying, chastising his body, and imploring the mercy of heaven; except a few hours which he devoted to making every sort of wicker-work, which he sold for the profit of the poor. He was always ready to oblige others, and always active in mortifying himself; and if his crimes had been numerous, horrid, bloody, his penance was now severe, frightful, and uninterrupted. The monk to whom he had trusted his awful secret, the true cause of his voluntary sufferings, has assured me since that of all the conversions which heaven had allowed him to be a witness of, none had astonished and moved him so much as that of this wretched man.

"If you had seen him," added he, "you would have felt your soul sink within you. He passed often a whole week without touching any food, never slept but when slumber forced down his emaciated body on the wet earth of his miserable hut, and ceased not to give himself up to convulsive terrors. His cheeks had been furrowed by his incessant tears. His body was lacerated by the many blows which he inflicted upon it, and a heavy chain riveted in two iron girths, the one of which was tightened around his breast, and the other twisted around his thighs, caused it to bend like a bow. He was willing to listen to such words of consolation or of mercy, as I uttered to him, believed that God would forgive him, and prayed with me for hours, but would never consent to remit his punishment, and took an incredible satisfaction in exhausting his body with the most cruel tortures he could imagine. Neither entreaties nor time were able to overcome this determination. He lived so for twenty-three years.

"Indeed, it is from such monuments of true repentance that we may understand," concluded the monk, "how a repentant sinner sometimes deserves the admiration of men, and obtains the pardon of heaven. I doubt not, but his judges would have been fully satisfied, if, like me, they had been able to contemplate, in that dreadful state of misery and unheard of sufferings, the man whom they had ordered to a scaffold, and whose escape had irritated them so much. But, it was the will of Heaven that I alone should see and know this secret. I can tell it now, according to his own wishes, that it may serve for the instruction of man. But who he was, and where he was condemned, I never knew, nor did I ever ask him to confess it to me."

The monk was right. Names in such cases are of no use; nay, it should be desirable for the sake of those families, of whom one member offends and is legally punished, that his name was never known. When a criminal repents, and is forgiven or liberated, his name should cease to be a cause of dishonour.

Some persons will say to that: the examples, like the one reported above, are rare. I confess it. But they must confess also, that there are very few men who are as guilty as that one was. Regret, repentance, expiation can be but in proportion to the crime which causes them.

My object is not to deny the fact, that great criminals do not commonly repent, but merely to show that true repentance is possible; and, therefore, that it is rational to demand, first of all, that the feelings of a family be spared whenever the law is forced to punish, and, secondly, that the power of forgiving should never be effaced from the code of a well governed nation.

If that power is improperly placed in the hands of a king, a president, a governor, or any other class of an executive, because an individual is liable to error, and, sometimes to a dangerous partiality; let that power abide either in a jury sworn for the purpose, or in the very legislature of the State to which the convict belongs; but try not to do away with it, because it is ordered by nature, and, as I have said, nature cannot be destroyed though it may be neglected or even violated for a time.

Men, I doubt not, will, sooner or later, acknowledge that such of their laws as sanction the execution of murderers on a scaffold, are an evident usurpation of the eternal power, and, consequently, will repeal them through obedience to that power: but also, they never will forget that the right of punishing which they have, is founded, before all, upon the power of revising their sentences which may either be unjust or too severe; and, therefore, the right of forgiving will always stand in the very centre of society, as an indestructible monument of its celestial origin.

THE END.

New Orleans Scottish Rite College

http://www.youtube.com/c/NewOrleansScottishRiteCollege

Clear, Easy to Watch
Scottish Rite and Craft Lodge
Video Education

Made in the USA
Monee, IL
04 November 2026

67377556R00121